MW01198947

"Williams makes a journe
posts along the way. His
us as we each awaken. We understand that thing.....
actualized. I read this book in one day, feeling more uplifted with
every page! This is destined to be a best-seller in these times of
change. Having known Robert for over 25 years, I can say that he
truly lives his Light."

– Jonette Crowley
Author of *The Eagle and the Condor* and *Soul Body Fusion*®

"Love is the Power is a truly amazing account of Robert O.
Williams' journey from his unique childhood experiences to
becoming the inventor of groundbreaking technology. Robert clev-
erly explains his awakenings and the gifts that lead him to creating the Heart+ App and this book, which together are a blueprint
for world peace by incorporating love, science and technology."

– Pat Cash
Wimbledon Men's Singles Champion, Charity Campaigner,
Life Mentor, father of four, grandfather of two

"Robert Williams' timely book (and new app) is just what the doctor
ordered to help us navigate the waters of stressful uncertainty."

– Barnet Bain
Director of *Milton's Secret*, Author of *The Book of Doing and Being:
Rediscovering Creativity in Life, Love and Work*

"Do you love that feeling when you're let in on a big secret? The
more I read of *Love is the Power*, the bigger it felt! It is clear now
that Robert Williams was divinely guided on his mission to provide
a technology that improves the life of every living creature on the
planet. So good, it was literally "to die for" – very grateful he came
back to write this valuable book that everyone will enjoy reading."

– Stephen Powers, CEO, BodhiTree.com

"*Baraka* is an ancient word defining the beneficent force of God flowing into aspects of creation worthy of enjoying His holy presence. Robert awakens us to a different reality extending God's divine *Baraka* to you in *Love is the Power*. In this manifesto, your love will come alive, and in this love, you will find the joy of God. In this joy of God, you find God within yourself. I encourage all to join Robert on his ascended journey to heal the heart of humanity."

– Joe Heller, Harmonic Evolution

"A fascinating life story that spans being a musician on stage with the *Beach Boys* to becoming the creator of Quantum Code Technology. *Love is the Power: One Man's Journey to Heal the Heart of Humanity* is truly a great read, filled with pure heart, spiritual awakenings and true life experiences. Robert O. Williams' hope for humanity is beautiful. This book must be shared."

– Temple Hayes
Spiritual Leader, Author, Difference Maker

"Robert dedicated his life and life's work to bring us to the leading-edge through – *Love is the Power*. Whilst seemingly a topic of infinite commentary, Robert's work shows its simplicity. It may just be time to lean in and surrender. The hearts of the world need us."

– Natalie Cook
OAM 5-Time Olympian, Gold and Bronze Medalist/Beach Volleyball

---

"Robert is a heart-awakening visionary who has given us the codes to bring forth the dawn of our collective planetary healing and transformation of human consciousness. The quantum leap we have all been waiting for..."

– Dr. Daniel B. Taylor, OMD

"Love is the power and is the message from a man who has gone through more than most of us could dream of, and what a journey. Robert's experience is both unthinkable and incredible, and to think he found a way for us to heal the world on his travels. With the way we are destroying the planet and ourselves don't you think it's time to step back and embrace the Quantum Codes and the power they possess to heal ourselves and in turn heal the planet? I dare you to read the book and try not to get involved in healing the world. I'm all in."

– Matt Pini
Dual International Rugby Union Player representing
Australia and Italy in the World Cup

"From *The Beach Boys* to beached-out bliss, Robert Williams' soul journey is remarkable and inspirational. And it's more – it's a reminder to all of us who we really are. This little miracle of a book is something to return to again and again, especially in those moments when we forget."

– Bryan Hubbard
Co-editor, *What Doctors Don't Tell You* and Author of *The Untrue Story of You*

"Robert O. Williams has had an incredible life experience. I'm so grateful he shared it with us in his new book, *Love is the Power*. His connection to source energy has pulled him through some rough challenges. He emerged through it all like a butterfly and his invention gives us hope for humanity. This book is a must read. I highly recommend it, five stars!"

– Catherine Lanigan
Author of *Angel Watch, Divine Nudges, Angel Tales, Romancing the Stone, The Jewel of The Nile* and over 40 other best selling books

"Robert's Near Death Experiences (NDE) and the expanded spiritual journey that resulted will resonate with many people. Robert came back for the greater good of mankind. This book and his Heart+ App invention will make a difference in the consciousness of humanity at a time when we need it the most."

– Robert Gourlay
RFD, B.AS., M.AS., Research Scientist and Inventor

"Robert's book is more important now than ever. To have invented the Heart+ App to help shift global mass consciousness and invite our participation in the 1% Challenge is genius!"

– Deirdre Hade
Spiritual Teacher, Healer, Author of
The (not so) Little Book of Surprises

LOVE IS THE POWER

One Man's Journey
to Heal the Heart of Humanity

Robert O. Williams

One08 Publishing Company, Inc.

333 S. State St., Lake Oswego, Oregon 97034 USA

Copyright © 2017, One08, Inc.

First edition. All rights reserved, including the right to reproduce this book or portions thereof in any form whatsoever without prior written permission.

ISBN-13: 978-1542751148

ISBN-10: 1542751144

Table of Contents

Foreword

This book is a revolution. It accomplishes what every great revolution seeks – to change the way we look at our relationships, our lives, and the very world we live in. It answers some of the deepest questions that have haunted us since the very beginning of time – who are we and why are we here? Most importantly, it gives us a glimpse into the near future when a small but critical number of people reach the same conclusion – that contrary to what we've been told we are not weak and vulnerable, but powerful beyond our wildest imaginations.

Maybe it sounds impossible, but these are not ungrounded, wishful ideas. In fact, most of them have been proven beyond any doubt. The only difference is that now, at last, science is catching up with what we've always known to be true. After decades of research and hundreds of studies we know that it does not take a majority of the population adopting an idea to begin the inevitable shift toward that idea's realization. In fact, as Robert shares with us in *Love is the Power*, we now know that if one percent of humanity passionately accepts a new idea or way of being, the momentum created by that group is enough to catapult it into reality. Past generations called them miracles, but as we begin to realize, then practice the technology behind these happening, what once seemed like a miracle becomes a way of life.

I've had the opportunity to witness this many times in my own life. I've had the opportunity to travel to many countries enduring great conflicts and war to perform a concert made up of the peace prayers from the world's great religions, and each time I encouraged people to join me by meditating at the same time the concert took place. For example, in 1998 I was invited to perform the concert in Baghdad by Saddam Hussein at a time when renewed violence seemed certain. It was the first time a synchronized meditation of this sort had been conducted, but by the time the concert began millions of people responded by stopping what they were doing for fifteen minutes and sending their energy and prayers to Iraq. I could feel the shift, and three days later, against all expectations, a peace accord was signed. They said it was a miracle, but we knew better.

You can say that it was just a coincidence, but I could tell story after story that begins and ends the same way. The fact is simple – when massive numbers of people focus passionately on a single idea, the universe bends to accommodate.

That brings us to the subject of this book. Robert has harnessed and perfected a quantum technology over many years of research and has used what he learned to validate the hundreds of studies demonstrating the power of mass collective consciousness. He has a single goal in mind – to move humanity from the current stranglehold of fear to a tangible experience of love leading to world peace. And now for the best news of all – the entire answer can be programmed into an app that can be used by nearly every person on this planet. The Heart+ App uses Quantum Code Technology and Robert shares here how it works and the science behind how it can lower stress and open our hearts, just by running it on our smart phones. The best part is you can join the 1% Challenge as you use the app, helping shift our world from fear to love.

You were guided to this book – I'm sure of it – just as I'm sure that you are not on this planet at this moment in history by accident. You are here to be part of the most revolutionary shift in human consciousness since we discovered fire. The truth is we've discovered a new kind of fire, one that has the potential to burn through the separating patterns and beliefs that have held us captive for a very long time. And that fire is inside each and every one of us, if only we would have the courage to unleash its power. That moment has at last arrived, and One08 is the first step toward the unveiling of a new world. Will you choose to be part of it? Luckily for all of us, you already have, just by reading this book.

– James Twyman
Peace Troubadour, NY Times Best Selling author of fifteen books, has recorded over eighteen albums and has produced or directed six films

Dedication

To two people who always reflect the
Highest Power of Love back to me – my wife
Karie Kristen, and my daughter Briella Amma

Acknowledgments

When I reflect upon my own individual location within the blossoming of humanity and in the writing of this book, creating a list of acknowledgments seems an impossible task. Thoughts, ideas, inspirations, realizations, and all other factors involved in this beautiful process are, and must be, a collective phenomenon. In those moments after I returned to life in March of 1979, it was as if all of YOU were teaching me. You have never stopped.

To you now reading these words, and to all of you collectively, thank you.

There have also been some stars who have stood out during the night times of my soul, who continue to evoke my deep personal gratitude. Those people include Michael Kelly for his decades of vision, perseverence, development and grounding the practical platforms to unite our yearning hearts together. To Bo Rinaldi for his recognition of the profundity of those platforms and for all his advice and wisdom in the writing of this book, and to Star Rinaldi for her Light behind Bo's abilities and skills. To Dr. Daniel Taylor for his beautiful spirit and his profound medical knowledge. To Clifford Schinkel for his amazing artistic abilities of editing, layout, and design.

If there is such a thing as a twin soul, then Patti Leach fits that concept completely in my life. The inspiration and guidance I receive from her is endless. In addition to my wife Karie, my daughters Briella and Patti give me the true power of love in the practical here and now.

To Lahiri Mahasaya, Paramahansa Yogananda, Swami Brahmananda Saraswati, Maharishi Mahesh Yogi, Charlie Lutes, Mata Amritanandamayi, Sri Sri Ravi Shankar, Beautiful Painted Arrow (Joseph Rael), Malidoma Patrice Somé, Barbara and Jack Pennington, Mohammed Abdalbaki, Jon and Dennette Ramos, Father Walter Klimchuck, Adi Da Samraj, and the saints and enlightened beings of the ages: for me you have proven that the love of power can truly be transformed to the Power of Love.

The science of today is merging with the wisdom of the ages, but not easily. It is only by the courage and commitment of the following scientists (and others I have yet to meet) to explore technologies against conventional agendas and largely without proper funding and support. It is from such visionaries and trail-blazers that throughout the ages science has grown to encompass not only the advancement of the digital age, of which we are all so profoundly living in, but of a digital age with companions from, and of, the heart of nature itself. I am humbled in my acknowledgments to personally thank the remarkable dedication and achievements from Beverly Rubik, PhD; William Tiller, PhD; Daniel Taylor, OMD; Harry Jabs, MS; Dean Radin, PhD; Karl Maret, MD; Beth McDougall, MD; Charles Palmer, MD; Dinesh Agraval, PhD; Tania Slawecki, PhD; Yury Kronn, PhD; David Henderson; Hiroshi Motoyama, PhD; Rupert Sheldrake, PhD; Daniel Benor, MD; Daniel Dunphy, PA; Steven Finkbine, PhD; James Oschman, PhD; Kim Jobst, DM; John Weeks, PhD; Iris Bell, MD; and the late Rustum Roy, PhD.

And to Mike Love, who trusted me during those times when I wasn't even visible to others to receive trusting.

– ROW

Prologue

In 1979 there was a period of about thirty minutes when I lost all abilities of my five senses: hearing, touch, sight, taste, smell. I also lost the conventional ability to think, feel emotion, and self-reflect.

There was Light during those minutes. Only Light. I use the word "light" loosely...not light from the sun or light bulbs, but Light (with a capital "L") as an infinite reality, greater than, and previous to any contrast or dualistic awareness of any kind. Before any movement.

This "Light" has not gone anywhere since then, but it dims when I think about it, write about it, or talk about it. With that caveat, I write this book. My second caveat is that I've done my best to "step aside."

> *Once certain technical know-how becomes our second nature, like writing or speaking, at some point in the creative process we learn to step aside allowing something much greater than our so called normal "self" to manifest. When we reflect back, we were most often in awe of these moments.*

So, I wrote in such a way in my journal. Sometimes the moments were spontaneous. Other times, I had to do something to find that opening. Either way, it was only during those moments that I wrote this book.

Backtrack with me for a second as you read. Right now, our eyes are passing over symbols. This is how it works from a "scientific" point of view:

1. The symbols were established about three thousand

years ago to represent certain sounds, vowels and consonants, etc. Symbols became "letters."

2. The letters combined with other letters to mimic sound variations, which the original humans who spoke English chose to develop and over time consistently agree upon.

3. Soon after your birth, you began to hear sounds, and each time you associated the sound with a meaning. Your mind took the audible impressions and created "files" which to draw upon later. The next time you heard similar sounds, you tapped into those files, and the memory of meaning became the dominant function of "your" mind in that moment.

4. In short, you were hearing words by sound waves vibrating your ear drums.

5. Then, because of the nature of the times in human evolution, symbols were strung together to form words. In time your brain associated each word with larger sentences. Those sentences were placed in front of your eyes and over time "files" were created for these also. Both your auditory and visual files were added to, referenced from, and reorganized each time somebody read a book to you.

6. In short, seeing words by light waves vibrating your retina, in turn stimulates certain nerves in your brain, and body. These vibrations, in turn resonate with similar vibratory sound impressions you learned earlier.

7. The files then conjure up information that your mind presents to your consciousness to interpret, react to, or ignore.

8. You were not born with "your mind." Your mind

was created as an intricate mechanism for information storage, retrieval, communication and even creative imagination. You found that you could actually change a memory at will, or add information via your imagination.

So the words you are seeing on the page of this book are being presented to your consciousness, which activates your mind for the above-mentioned reason.

There is a very thin layer of interference, a veil, or maybe we can even call it protection, between your mind and your consciousness. It's a veil nonetheless.

Poetry, music and art often trick the mind to let go of associating each word with something from the past.

So does pain, intense suffering, darkness and death.

Fortunately so does openness, presence and free awareness. Let's call this type of awareness "The Heart." Let's call the free exchange between our hearts and all that is arising, "Love." Let's call the intelligence governing the qualities of Love from the Heart, "Light." And let's call the effect of our freely open awareness making intelligent use of Love, "Power." Miracles happen with this type of power. It is power that has a built-in safety mechanism to ensure that ONLY miracles which are of the highest good for all things during this special time of earth...will happen. The Power is based in the Whole Intelligence of the Universe.

Our minds cannot understand this but they will try. Observe the mind's efforts, and then observe the moments when the mind loses its hold to something greater...closer to what I am calling, Love.

Our Hearts have always understood it fully without any effort whatsoever.

On March 20th, 1979, whether you were born or not, wherever you were, whatever you were doing, WE experienced a thirty minute event.

We discovered that nothing is isolated and alone. From each sub-atomic particle to the Universe itself, everything is connected, and information is constantly being *exchanged* from one reality to another...a kaleidoscope of diversity always connected to everything else.

You – we – I have been asking three things over and over in a million different ways during this time on Earth. And these are:

Who am I? Who are we? What is our purpose?

If we are fortunate enough to have allowed these questions to remain a mystery, and feel that for now, Love is our Purpose, no matter what we're doing from day to day. And if we feel that through our Hearts we can tap into an incredible vast reservoir of energy, then indeed Love is the Power.

The Power for what? We all know the answer. We know that things can be better for life on this earth. Some of us may have settled for less, but deep down we know it can be better. We just haven't figured out exactly how to use Love in a powerful enough way to affect every human being on this planet.

I am writing this book because I have absolutely no doubt that we have enough people on this planet, right now, to make a difference. A transformation from one fundamental paradigm to another is already in process. The Universe and Nature on this planet are doing that regardless of what we do. What we need to do is simply locate ourselves as part of Nature itself. There is a natural law, which says that if a certain percentage of the fundamental parts of any system align in a particular way, the entire system will quickly transform itself making the system more coherent. It is a simple act of quantity and alignment, an almost mechanical use of biological laws, yet the collective act of even a small percentage of people can have a miraculous impact on the foundation for all human life. Some have called this time, the "Time of Awakening." Love is the Power and with love as we have defined it above, we can enhance the already in-process transformation.

One of the first experiences I had as an individual consciousness after the time of complete Light, was understanding the developmental phase we are now living as human beings. More profoundly I understood what the next highest level of evolution could be for humanity and the planet at large.

My prayer is that this book serves you in some way for *your* next highest level of Good – your next phase of incarnation – your location in the blossoming of humanity. No matter what though, our unity in Love will be collectively realized as the truth prior to and completely enveloped within the service of you as a unique and gifted single human being.

Our opportunity is to realize this reality sooner than later.

The key is understanding that Love is the Power.

Chapter 1:
BIRTH OF A BODY

The hospital alarms had gone off. There was no turning back now. The alarms and hysteria were because a baby had been born and it wasn't breathing, even after the standard slap on the butt. The fear in the room was that this new human being would become one of those tragic and mysterious "still-born" or "blue babies."

Suddenly, the baby gasped and cried. The blue color quickly disappeared.

The baby was named Robert Odus Williams. Years later I would become familiar with the other names and other bodies I had occupied. Most relevant to this book "I" became familiar, not as a body, personality, or ego being, but as a *tabula rasa,* a "blank slate" of receptive observation. I observed how the veils work between life and death, between dreaming and waking, between the physical world and the spiritual worlds. Most fascinating...is observing the veils between people... between you and me.

> *Right now there is no ultimate difference between you, me and we. The symbols which make up the words _will_ make it seem that you are "there" reading and "I" have written the words previously. This is true only at a very small micro pinpoint in the Whole of Truth.*

So I was born Robert Odus Williams on July 1, 1954 at 5:36PM in Oakland, California and, like most of us, would succumb into the amnesia factor, forgetting at least temporarily, all the previous identities I had taken.

My earliest memories in this life were not of "me" being "me" as a baby or child, but as some kind of consciousness observing the little baby crawling, the child eating, clinging, laughing and crying.

I also remember seeing things that my parents and others (because they couldn't see them) claimed were solely in my imagination, and therefore not real. I remember only seldom being completely identified with my bodily existence. Even when I saw things physical through my physical eyes, there was something else bigger behind me, that was observing.

When I became most associated with my physical body was in times of emotional trauma or physical pain. Later in my life, I became grateful for these times as they forced me to incarnate. It took me a long time, but I discovered that our current bodies are like holy temples that, collectively are going through a major make-over. All of our bodies are being upgraded. Let us not forget that every elemental particle which our bodies are made of came from the earth. In other words, all of our bodies put together are just as much a part of the earth as what's deep inside, under the surface. When we say the earth is changing, so are our bodies. Are we ONLY our bodies? No. And neither is the earth "only" the earth.

> The earth is being cradled by many forces beyond the human minds' capacity to understand. However, the cradling fields and forces are as a loving mother is to her crying child.

In my early years most of the time the "I" was an observer of many worlds, although in a way, connected to the earth at all times.

I would become intimately familiar with the mechanics of the birthing and dying processes, and would travel through the death portal and then trace back the links to my current body, mental impressions and emotional patterns – the Robert reality. So in a sense, the "I was born on July 1st..." statement is grossly incomplete. I have died and been born many times. But...this book is about *this* lifetime for me and *your current* lifetime for you.

Chapter 2
JING

Almost every day I would go to the back yard. I had always seen the spinning beings – often called "nature spirits." In the back yard I could be with them freely. None of my other friends could see them when I pointed them out, so I resisted being with other boys and girls in the neighborhood.

I remember I had begun digging down into the sandbox, just far enough so I could lay there about halfway submerged. Looking up at the sky, I listened to the bird and insect sounds, feeling absolutely comfortable.

The nature spirits were always pretty much doing their own thing. Sometimes they would come close to me and hover above me with their innocent curiosity for a moment or two as I lie in my sandbox, only to flitter away back to the trees, bushes and plants.

I wanted to keep digging in the sandbox but was afraid my father would disapprove. His anger was pretty much constant, but much less toward me personally during these early years, while focusing on my older sister and my dear mom who were regularly subject to it.

For me he was much more allowing and even exceptionally kind and loving. I was "his son" which he had so wanted.

I asked him if I could keep digging down into the sandbox into the moist dirt below. Surprisingly, he seemed pleased when I asked and even showed me where to pile the dirt so as to not make a mess. "Dig here, pile there."

I couldn't stop digging. Being on my hands and knees was my constant daily routine. Every day for at least an hour or so I would dig, pile and lay down to stare outward. I loved watching the spinning beings while lying in my hole.

One day my father came home with a small shovel, fit for a boy my age - about five or six years. Where he got such a wonderful gift for me I don't know; I don't remember seeing these in the hardware store which I would venture to regularly for supplies to build my fort years later.

I coveted that shovel. It was "mine" – a gift of manhood from my tall, tough, war hero father. So amazing he was to me. He simply let me dig. I loved him.

It became a ritual. I would play with our two black lab mutts for a few minutes, and then would move to the far end of the back yard where my hole "in-process" was waiting. The whole area – my hideout – separated the sand from the rest of the world – the sand and dirt already beginning to look obvious against the back fence where my father said I could pile it.

The shovel, the sand and dirt, and the lying down ritual after my digging arms gave out. The sky, the birds, the trees, plants and the beings. And then one wonderful morning...Jing.

He was so playful and happy, and unlike the other nature spirits was looking right at me with a wise and loving smile. He knew me. He was about five feet tall – much taller than I was – and dressed in green, yellow and purple. I was instantly comfortable with him and he soon became my constant playmate and teacher in my backyard world.

Sometimes he would simply dance delightfully for me. Skipping, spinning and jumping from side-to-side. Often in the middle of the dance he would suddenly stop and motion me toward something in the yard...a snail for instance.

The natural world is completely diverse. No two members of this world are exactly alike. Yet there are a handful of Universal Laws which every single animal, insect and plant abide. They are blueprints and codes that the creatures of the earth are always resonating with, and therefore, always governed by.

Take the snail for instance. The snail's slimy body conforms with one of the most profound and ubiquitous geometric ratios. The "phi" ratio, also where the "golden mean" comes from.

The snail's spiral shell grows exactly in accordance with the golden mean. Exactly. Every single snail that's ever been on this earth – grew this way.

Our back yard had many snails since more than half was almost constantly in the shade. Jing would direct me to simply watch how a snail moved, the stream of fluid it would leave in its trail, and most importantly it seemed, the shell itself. He would point and smile. I would look and if my gaze was not intent enough, he would point again and again until he felt I "got it."

One time he hastened me to the front yard where my mom had the sprinkler on – one of those back and forth kind. At some point in the watering cycle, a beautiful rainbow would briefly appear. This is what Jing was so excited about and when the rainbow appeared he would joyfully dance and gesture.

The natural world never shows all of its possibilities at once. The natural world <u>reveals</u> itself based upon cycles, phases and conditions. For instance, rainbows are always there but only reveal themselves when water and the sun are aligned just right.

It is a mistake to think that the water and sun created the rainbow.

Rainbows are always there.

All things we are seeking are always already there but because of our state of consciousness, we haven't allowed them to appear. Ultimately, we let go of all our efforts to create them on our own – to control them – to find them – to see them.

Our attitude of searching, seeking and achieving will reveal very little.

During this time of Earth, things begin to effortlessly appear relative to our state of consciousness.

At other times, Jing would point to the clouds and when my attention would wander, he would wave his arms to keep me looking in the right direction again, until I "got it." The way the clouds formed followed certain patterns of regularity. He also seemed to teach me about the weather and the seasons and how the nature spirits changed their behavior.

Jing was the only being that I had a one-on-one, direct relationship with. There was a kind of a hierarchy of size and intelligence ranging from extremely small spins around the grasses, such as bugs and worms, to the grand beings of the trees. The larger the tree the larger the being. We had two mid-size trees in the back yard. The beings in and around them would often look at me more intently than the smaller beings on the grass for instance, but only for a few seconds and never leave their posts in and around their trees.

Jing on the other hand, would follow me even to school sometimes – about three blocks away. As soon as I became involved with other students though, he would most often leave. I don't think he went far though. Since I was a mischievous child, I would often find myself in desperate situations, some even life threatening, and an adult would inevitably find and help me.

There was a creek about a block away from our house with

one of those claw fences. Usually I was able to scoot myself under the fence to venture down to the creek to play, and often I collected buckets full of little frogs. I would bring them back and let them loose in the back yard only to be told by my mom or dad to round them all up and return them to the creek.

One morning I got stuck on the underside of the claw fence. If I scooted forward a part of the fence would jab me in my side; if I scooted back the same part would jab me in the neck. I tried desperately to wiggle myself out, but the more I tried the more the fence dug into me. At one point I simply gave up and started crying for help. Out of the side of my eye I saw Jing. It only took a few moments before a woman driving by pulled over, spotted me and helped me out.

Yet another time, I somehow got stuck in the backyard swing set. I was shimmying up the chain link from the side bar to one of the swings, when I slipped and dangled with the chain right around my neck. I was holding the side bar with my left foot only. Had I slipped further, I would have strangled myself. I couldn't speak; the chain was so tight around my neck. Again I saw Jing, and within a minute my mother – who normally left me alone for hours in the back yard without concern – rushed out to save me. Later she recalled, she "just had a feeling" she should check on little Bobby. "Mother's intuition" she thought – which I'm sure was true – but I also knew Jing had something to do with it.

By the time I was eleven the hole was almost six feet deep and five feet wide. I knew this because my dad, who was just over six feet tall, proudly stood in the hole and held out his arms. He was proud of my accomplishment and even suggested that in case of a nuclear attack, we could use the hole as a fall-out shelter for the family. I then built a wooden "roof" over the hole and started stocking the "shelter" with Campbell's Soup and other canned foods. Once I was finished with the shelter, I began building "Fort Obey" on the side of the house with wooden planks I got from my grandmother's garage (for some reason she had all kinds of wood in there) and aluminum sheets she got from some friend of hers who worked on a newspaper's printing press.

Jing was with me every day while I constructed the fort with one large "room" and a long enclosed "hallway" with a little peephole on the side facing my hole and part of the back yard. One "wall" was the side of the house. I loved it when it rained and I snuggled at the end of the hallway looking out my peephole, listening to the rain sounds on the tin roof. Sometimes Jing would dance and perform joyfully while I watched him from my shelter. He was never worried about getting "wet" in the rain.

One summer my family went to the Redwood Forest. That experience opened me up to a world I had never before imagined, even with the spirits and Jing around my house in San Lorenzo, California.

At many points during my childhood, I would go into a state where I couldn't easily speak. I certainly didn't want to. Speaking would interfere with what I was observing most of the time. Our trip to the Redwood Forest was one I will never forget.

The mighty Redwoods were so alive, sublime and wise. Even my parents and sister were quiet as we strolled through the forest looking at some tree trunks over twenty feet in diameter and over two-hundred feet tall. The beings I saw in and around these trees were almost too much for me to take in and keep breathing at the same time. They were just like their physical forms – tall, strong and mighty – but in the spirit world, so much more.

I noticed that at the same time they were welcoming us and delighting in our admiration of them, they were also warning us. It took me years to understand their warnings, but at that time I was simply spellbound.

I couldn't speak, nor did I have any reason to. The trees had captured all of my attention. My body went through the necessary activities of a child – getting dressed, eating, drinking, going to the bathroom and so on – but there was no desire for anything else. I would simply sit in my room remembering them, or perhaps better stated, "I was still *with* Them."

> *All forms of physicality respond to all that is changing from moment to moment. The sun, the moon, the stars, the weather and the fluctuating magnetic fields all affect our physical reality. Some changes occur in billionths of a second, while others occur once every multi-billion years.*
>
> *Over the last hundred years, the collective intuitions of humans have aligned more than ever before. We have all been intuiting radical change; we have been sensing the season upon us.*
>
> *A radical transformation of the earth and all its inhabitants is inevitable. How things will look on the other side of this transformation is not inevitable. In fact, we have been obliged to participate, both individually and more important- ly, together…in the transformation itself. Our participation WILL affect the outcome. It will only take a few of us with Hearts awakened just a bit more to make a huge difference. We are at The Threshold.*
>
> *Humans have been given free will. They have been given the gift of co-creating the outcome of inevitable change. Most of the earthly changes will be automatic under the governance of natural laws, but a critical component of that change will be a function of human consciousness and our free will gift.*

Trees are like carrier waves of awareness with "wide angle" lenses that can look at large spans of time. They are currently broadcasting information about an opportunity for human consciousness, which all humans feel at some level.

After not speaking for three days, my mother became concerned and brought me to Dr. Vrabel. "He's become deaf and mute," she exclaimed.

"Bobby, can you hear me?" The doctor looked me straight in the eye. I stared back still only seeing the Redwoods.

Then she carefully lifted my arm and began tickling me right in the spot where we all tickle. I finally broke my silence, first with a giggle and then an outburst of laughter. I popped out of my trance state. Smart doctor!

Chapter 3

THE FORSAKEN ONE

One day Jing came to me with the saddest expression I had ever seen on him. I asked him what was the matter. Of course he didn't answer. He had never spoken; he simply bowed and bid me farewell.

Gone.

I cried and cried, alone in my fort. The nature spirits were still there, the birds, the snails and our dogs. But I was so alone, more than I had ever been up to that point.

In so many ways, I discovered that the experience of Jing served me well. I was able to experience nature and the miraculous phenomenon that if we notice or not, what is occurring is occurring in and around us always.

In hindsight I can say at least that when Jing left I was experiencing the loss of my preadolescent innocence. I had noticed a different feeling within my body; my muscles were more firm; my voice was crackling and I took on a different energetic relationship with girls. What was this odd attraction, fascination and...fear?

When Jing left my anger grew as well. My previous "home," – the back yard, my hole (now over six feet deep), the plants and even the trees – had lost their luster. The luster would come back but not for several years. I still saw the beings in nature, but less vividly. I began to notice humans and their behaviors more intently. Nevertheless, it took me years to get over the loss of Jing.

> *Part of the human destiny is for the mind, body and*
> *emotions (the "self") to lose everything. All that had been*

consoling to our self-identities must depart.

The mind field of each human being is a great gift but only to a certain point. At that point, the very mind which defined ourselves – and even helped us to survive our egos – becomes the greatest enemy to The Light – to the truth of who we really are.

Light doesn't exclude any of those comfortable or satiating things we can experience. In fact, all those things become just as full and complete as the Light itself. There ultimately is no separation.

But until this is Realized, there is a grand attempt by the mind to understand and control everything. It draws from all experiences and impressions, categorizing them in memory banks: 1) things that feel good, 2) things that feel bad, and 3) everything in between.

The Light – You – will only accept these categories for so long. Eventually, the YOU will either disrupt or entirely remove the limited realities of the self, simply because they are not your ultimate life.

I was eleven or twelve most likely. The nights also became longer. My mother told me later in life that almost every time she would check on me at night, I was awake.

I remember wondering how my parents, sister and everyone else would get through the night without concern. For me, when the lights went out the world in my mind would simply light up. I would go to bed around eight o'clock and remain awake until my parents would turn off the TV, after a midnight late-show such as Johnny Carson. Then I'd hear them shuffle around, flush the toilets and finally turn out their bedroom light, which I could still see a bit in the crack between the bottom of my bedroom door and the floor.

The night carried on and I wondered how they could just lay

there in bed and not be bored. I was very bored. I would get up and play with my erector set or whatever else just to pass the time. Sometimes I would slip into an unconscious mode – sleep – but not for very long. Usually the sun would start rising before any rest would happen.

It was only after I was eleven or twelve that I became aware that I was always awake. I told my mother, who upon hearing how my typical night was, brought me to Dr. Vrabel, who diagnosed me as a child insomniac and gave my mom some kind of drug to give me "if my sleep didn't improve."

I don't remember how long she gave me the sleeping pills exactly, only that by the time I went to high school, they had stopped.

It was during these years that I became aware of the many aspects of my health which didn't match those of my family or friends...constant allergies, sneezing, itching, poor digestion, constant sore throats, asthma, fevers and headaches. I was depressed most of the time, only to replace that with bouts of raging anger..."temper tantrums" as my mom called them.

What was there to not be angry at? My magical backyard world had become stale, the spinning spirits no longer interested me and my true companion and beloved confidant Jing, had left.

There were only two things that interested me now – girls and music.

The latter was easier.

My father had played in the army band during World War II. At first he played saxophone, but then switched to drums for the marching drills. His mother had purchased a small "soprano" saxophone when he was about seven because the local doctor thought it would help with his asthma.

My grandmother kept it for him and once he married my mom and they had me, it appeared in his closet.

In hindsight, my parents were very wise. Through my adolescent and teenage years I thought they knew very little about anything, but I was wrong. One example of their wisdom when I was seven myself, most likely shaped my destiny for many years to come.

My father would occasionally pull out the soprano sax and play it to my utter amazement. Of course I too wanted to play it right then and there, but my father refused me to even handle the horn – because I was too young.

When I turned six, my father allowed me only to press the keys down and up, but never to actually take the sax out of the case, put the mouthpiece on and play it.

When I turned seven that all changed. It was an initiation. My father set me down and ceremoniously took the saxophone out of the case, carefully put the mouthpiece on the neck, placed the small cane reed on the mouthpiece and blew a C scale. He gave me the horn and had me try.

Squeeeeeak.

He then pulled the mouthpiece off and blew into only that. A duck sound emitted. "Try that," he said.

After a few tries, I had mastered the duck sound. From there more sounds on the saxophone quickly ensued and my new escape had appeared.

I practiced relentlessly, learning a few war songs my father had remembered. It was time for lessons at a local music store.

Mr. Larmer was a lot bigger than my father, but kinder. He had a smile that I couldn't wait to see each week. Like my father, mother and every single adult I remember growing up around, he also smoked nonstop. The lessons were in a little room with no windows, just large enough for an upright piano.

For thirty minutes per week, I would progress through my "Lessons on Saxophone No. 1-10" book with Mr. Larmer pointing out new fingerings and rhythm notations. By the end of the lesson there was so much smoke in the room I could barely see. He would open the door dispersing the smoke only for me to get into our car – also full of smoke, and then my mom smoked all the way home, and on and on.

The fact that children of the 1950s have not all died of lung cancer speaks only to one of the many miracles of the human body.

> *After Light becomes, it allows the minds within the physical universe to try again. And again and again. It is inevitable that each time a mind begins to create a new reality, corresponding to pleasures, pain, achievements and loss, it will feel that "THIS TIME" it has figured life out. This new reality becomes the "new reason for living." It all begins to (supposedly) make sense. The self, blocked from The Light, wakes up from sleep and after a brief moment of mental reorganization via the memory, begins seeking the pleasure within its created reality and resisting the pain within that very same reality.*

> *These cycles sometimes continue for thousands of years.*

> *And then, to each of us when we are fortunate, all that the mind has created and held onto starts to break down or sometimes be totally removed from us. For the really fortunate, we reach a point where we stop fighting the breakdown. We realize that the more we try to get things back under control according to our created reality, the more difficult life becomes. We surrender to the process.*

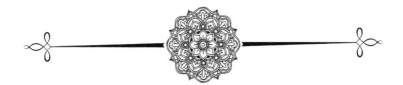

Chapter 4

MINDS ARE MADE TO BE BLOWN

The vocal harmonies were unmistakable, especially through the studio headphones that the horn players of *The Beach Boys* – including me – were using. The year was 1977 and through several miraculous events I landed a job playing sax for Brian Wilson, Mike Love and *The Beach Boys*.

I remember the first time I heard *Good Vibrations*, eleven years earlier. I was playing Ping-Pong with a neighbor. It was the fall of 1966, I was twelve years old and from *"I...I love the colorful clothes she wears,"* I was transfixed. I stopped playing Ping-Pong and ran to the transistor radio in the garage and stilled everything about myself to listen. When the song completed with the "alien helicopter cellos," as Brian later would call them, I turned off the radio. I didn't want to so easily forget what I had just heard.

www.youtube.com/watch?v=Eab_beh07HU

Back in those days if you missed the DJ announcing a song on the radio, you had to keep listening until you heard it again. Once you learned the title and saved up your money, the exciting trek to your local record store would follow. Sometimes records were sold at the five-and-dime store – but kept far in the back. "Devil music" wasn't to be too close to the kitchen knickknacks!

The top ten singles were usually displayed on the wall along with a dapper picture of the pop group. I paid fifty-nine cents for *Good Vibrations* and the side B instrumental, *Let's Go Away for a While.* Revolutionary! Both songs blew my mind every time I listened.

I think my "45 collection" was then up to a dozen, with half of them by *The Temptations*, my favorite group, and the King of Soul, James Brown. I played them a lot, but my secret favorites were not owned by me. They were the "78s" that my father had carefully stored under the Hi-Fi from the big bands of the 1930s and 1940s...Woody Herman, Glen Miller, Tommy Dorsey and Stan Kenton.

None of my friends would have anything to do with those records, calling the music "stupid," and my dad wouldn't let me play them without his supervision because they were *valuable*. After my mom, dad, and sister were asleep I would sneak to play them, with my right ear glued to the cloth dividing the huge twelve-inch Hi-Fi speaker from our living room.

By the time I got to junior high school *The Beach Boys* were simply not cool. Where I grew up in San Lorenzo, there were two distinct cliques...the "surfers" and the "gangs." Gangs weren't like they later became; they were just a bunch of guys who acted cool and would occasionally switch hubcaps on cars for fun. If someone got caught driving to school with one wrong hubcap they became the laughing stock of the student body, and everyone knew that it was one of the "gangsters" who did it. Surfers were too good to ever do such a thing.

I was a member of a gang called "The Blacks." Not because we were African-American, but because we all wore black nylon jackets. My initiation was to smoke an entire cigarette behind the backstops in the seventh grade. I did it by inhaling just enough smoke to settle in my mouth, breathing regular air in my nose with my throat closed, and blowing it out, which would prevent the smoke from getting into my lungs. I practiced for my initiation a few times after copping some cigarettes from my mother. Once, the smoke did get down into in my lungs and I coughed nonstop for what seemed like hours after.

I liked being in the gang because they didn't make fun of my two hideous-looking front teeth. I had broken my two upper front ones out of my mouth in the second grade. I was trying to impress a girl I had a crush on by swinging around on the monkey bars near her. I wound up slipping and falling on the metal bar – jamming my two front teeth into my upper palate. The year was 1961 and the dental industry had yet to figure out natural looking crowns, but had advanced from all silver or gold ones. The "advancement" was silver crowns with the middle part white. Kind of like a refrigerator door with a stainless steel frame. It looked absolutely hideous, but that was the best they could do.

In the gang we all had little things we were ashamed of. Either we were overweight, underweight, full of zits, our noses were too big or too small, or were simply angry as all hell because of our abusive fathers who survived World War II. For me it was my teeth.

We loved smarting off, but rarely had the guts to do anything more than that, much less fight anyone or do anything really bad. Those who did advanced to tougher gangs with switchblades, alcohol and worse.

"The Blacks" had strict codes of conduct including NO SURFER MUSIC!

So, I listened to *Good Vibrations* and *Let's Go Away for a While* in secret while my parents and sister slept. The thought never even came close to entering my mind that less than eleven years later I would be on stage with *The Beach Boys* playing their greatest hits, including of course the song that changed my life.

By the time I became a freshman in high school I had distanced myself from "The Blacks" and became more obsessed with music. During the summer prior to entering the ninth grade, I practiced my sax every day. It paid off.

The first day in the Arroyo High School Band ("A" period which began at 7:30AM), the music teacher, Mr. Phillips told the class to warm up and play anything we wanted – all of us at the same time. It was a good thing that the music wing was more than a hundred yards from the rest of the campus. This was Mr. Phillips' way of hearing the various degrees of music skills in his new concert and marching band.

Along with Mr. Phillips, at the front of the room were a few seniors who began drifting around the band and listening to each section...clarinets, flutes, trombones, trumpets, percussion (the most plentiful), French horns, tubas, and saxes.

In those days, all schools and all grades had music classes. For those "brains," as we called them, who wanted honors and special awards for their exceptional grades, extra credit was a must, and the easiest way to earn it was to join afterschool music clubs like the rally band or concert orchestra.

I immediately knew I was the best in the sax section if not the entire band, except for one guy on snare drum who could do rolls and flam-diddles faster than anybody I had ever heard on drums, with the exception of Buddy Rich of course.

Two of the seniors stood right behind me while I was blowing everything I could possibly think of in that ten minutes of "free playing"– every scale I knew – major, minor, whole tone and then songs I had memorized like *The Theme from Bonanza* and *Peter Gunn*.

At the end of class, the seniors came up to me while I was putting away my alto sax and asked me to come back after school for a meeting with them and Mr. Phillips.

That whole day I couldn't stop thinking about what the meeting could be about. I knew I would play first saxophone; Mr. Phillips had re-arranged the entire band in accordance with their talents right after the "free play." But what else did they want to see me for?

Maybe I had done something wrong or violated some grown-up high school code of conduct that angered the seniors. I was scared.

In general, at this age I was afraid of speaking to anyone about anything. I was kind of a stutterer, extremely self-conscious and awkward in social situations. I could never figure out how people spoke to each other with such ease. I observed how friends would see each other and just start talking. How did they know what to talk about?

"Hey Bob, how's it going?"

"Fine," would be all I could come up with.

Any attempt from anyone to carry on a conversation with me was fruitless. I defaulted to "Uh-huh," "Yes," "No," or "I don't know," but nothing more. It wouldn't take long for people to either think I was a bit retarded, or simply lose interest in me and move on. It was worst when I tried to carry on a conversation with a girl. That was pretty much impossible for me. I was so smitten by any girl that approached me, or by chance sat next to me in class, that the best I could do was look down at the floor or worse yet, say something completely stupid like, "This class is good, right?"

"What?" she would say, startled.

"I mean, this class *isn't* good, is it?"

She would roll her eyes and quickly begin conversing with someone else.

All during these school years I could see auras, but I just wasn't interested in them. I didn't really understand the differences between them, unless a really odd thing appeared. For example, one time in the eighth grade I had a serious crush on Linda Rodriguez...deep sensuous beautiful brown eyes, long dark hair and a smile I knew was made just for me. I was still a member of "The Blacks" during this time, and unbelievably she once wore my black coat for a day...kind of like a girl wearing a guy's varsity block, but much cooler. I thought this meant she loved me and would be my girlfriend, then marry me and have kids. She would also totally understand me, not have a problem with my teeth and love my saxophone playing. She would understand me! She was my first massive crush and I obsessed about her 24/7.

I knew it was going to be a slow process to convince her to marry me and more, so I wrote her poems, sent her secret love letters, and praised her at every chance. For the most part, even though she had worn my coat that one time, she seemed oblivious to me. I'd give her the gum I knew she liked after school and she'd just say, "Thanks" then immediately move away and start talking to her friends.

She was in my English class and sat a few desks in front of me to the right. On one particular day, I noticed this beautiful golden color in her aura right around her heart area. In addition, there was a fiery red glow lower down around her female organs and vagina.

I was so drawn to this I couldn't stop looking at it. I had no idea what else was going on in class and luckily the teacher didn't call on me for anything. Focus, focus, focus into the gold and red areas of Linda Rodriguez! She became agitated, and changed positions in her seat.

"She must be thinking of me," I thought! "She understands how we would make love – for both our first time – under the full moon, followed by me playing my saxophone in such soothing and romantic tones! How I would give to her, stroke her beautiful hair, and how she would hold me and kiss me..."

I saw her physical body right there, two rows up from me

in Mrs. Gerfall's English class, starting to fidget. She also crossed her legs and started rocking them. I knew she was thinking and fantasizing about me now for sure. My dear, dear Linda! You love me and I love you!!! The red in her aura got brighter and brighter. I was sweating.

Then she suddenly turned around and looked right at me, but it was no look of love. It was the angriest look I had ever seen on a girl.

"STOP LOOKING AT ME," she screamed! The whole class was silenced and the teacher immediately rushed over and asked, "What's going on here?"

"Bob won't stop looking at me!"

The teacher slammed her hand on my desk and scolded, "Do *not* ever harass a girl, Bob!"

Right in front of everyone – now staring at me with livid eyes – the teacher changed my seat to the far back corner and told me that if she ever heard from *any girl* that I was harassing them, I would be expelled. I tried to speak out that I wasn't harassing her (whatever that meant), but that I loved her; I wanted to protect her and serve her! I couldn't say anything though. My throat was clogged.

This was the 1960s and although in the San Francisco Bay area women were well underway to becoming fully "liberated," had already burned their bras and proclaimed sexual equality...teachers and terrified parents were still fiercely protective of their girl students and daughters, including Mrs. Garfall, my English teacher. Plus I was one of those "Blacks" and she knew I was bad and up to no good.

I knew Linda didn't have eyes in the back of her head. I knew she had felt me. It was my first lesson in the use of subtle psychic energies for selfish reasons. Thoughts are energy and all energy has power. I *was* harassing her – I just didn't know it or understand what she was feeling. The gold in her aura was the Love I was able to access even at that age, yes, but the red was my lust. My selfish desire was natural at that age surely, but I had yet to learn the laws of how to rightly use psychic power.

As soon as I got home after school that day I practiced my saxophone late into the night. Music was not only the world which replaced Jing and my celestial friends in the back yard years ago, but it was also my escape.

As usual, I would "go to bed" at about 9:00PM and just lie there until my parents and sister went to bed. As soon as the TV and lights were off and I heard the final flush of the toilets for the night, I'd sneak out to the living room Hi-Fi.

I didn't listen to *Good Vibrations* that night. *"I...I love the color-ful clothes she wears..."* reminded me too much of Linda and the fool I had made of myself that day. I played *Malagueña* by The Stan Kenton Big Band over and over again.

https://www.youtube.com/watch?v=TN9sp6ApX4o

I concentrated on every phrase and every note until the sun started to rise the next morning and I had to prepare for school once again. This time, I was very careful with the use of my mind. Every girl I saw, I just sent them what I later learned was unconditional love. I really didn't want to hurt anyone or worse, be made a fool of in front of others.

Now back to the first day at high school – the "Concert Band," "A" period, Mr. Phillips and the two seniors...my stomach was in knots by the time the final bell rang and I was racing over to the music room.

I walked in and saw some kids milling around. They glanced at me and snarled. Mr. Phillips had a private office. The door was closed and he was inside talking on the phone.

I was so scared I felt like I was going to throw-up while I waited. Everything at high school seemed so big, so large and so overwhelming. About fifteen minutes later that feeling would take literal form.

Mr. Phillips finished his phone call, saw me out of his window and broke into a smile.

"Come on in, Bob!"

Wayne and Kory, the seniors who had asked me to come back after school, had been sitting behind Mr. Phillips and emerged also with smiles, but more serious ones.

"We'd like you to play baritone saxophone in the *Stage Band.* Usually, you have to be at least a junior to join that band, but Kory here wants to play guitar. He's been our Bari player up to now," Wayne said.

Mr. Phillips without hiding his excitement chimed in, "I've spoken to your parents and just got off the phone with Principal Jenkins. Right now you have 'Art' for your first period (part of the regular curriculum), and to change to '*Stage Band*' we first need the okay from your parents and Mr. Jenkins. They've okayed it, so now the decision is yours."

I was stunned and totally amazed. The reason why it was called the *Stage Band* was because they performed *on stage* at various events around San Lorenzo and the San Francisco East Bay, and even took an annual trip to the Reno Jazz Band Festival to compete in the largest high school jazz band competition in the United States. Throughout the early 1960s, the *Arroyo High School Stage Band* consistently came in first place. Over the last few years, as their star seniors graduated and left for college, the band slipped a few notches but Mr. Phillips was able to keep them at least in the top ten out of over a hundred schools from across the county. He was a great music teacher and had played jazz tenor saxophone

26

himself while growing up.

"Here's my Bari-sax," said Kory.

Kory pulled the huge horn out of the case, slowly assembled the pieces and blew a few notes. He hesitated, quickly glanced at his guitar in the corner, then back down to his Bari which he was still holding. He slowly unsnapped the neck strap and handed the massive horn to me.

It was as if such a thing – giving a Bari-sax to a young, wet-behind-the-ears freshman for the *Stage Band* – had never been done in the history of humanity. The three of them looked at me tentatively.

The size of this horn was about three-quarters as big as I was. Did I have the lungs to blow such a thing? I had been playing alto – a lot smaller – since the fifth grade having graduated from soprano, which was even smaller.

But now was my time. I blew *Peter Gunn* loud and clear and didn't miss a beat or a note.

I was in. The next day after Band, my first period was *Stage Band*! I would never learn about how to draw a vase or anything else for that matter. Art and painting were out; that would be my sister's profession. I was a musician now. I was in the *Arroyo Stage Band*!

Little would I know that the sounds I heard and felt while playing in this group and the experiences in Reno, Nevada later that year would pave the way for my meeting Mike Love and becoming a sax player member of *The Beach Boys* only nine years later.

My sax, my new family and my practice sessions replaced Jing.

> *Our good feelings, our good radiance, our loving, tend to appear when our circumstances are comforting to us. When we have met consolation and we "know" what life is all*

about, at least for that moment, then we feel okay enough, even obliged at times, to give to others, to be kind and compassionate and to offer love. Once our circumstances change, our tendencies to give to others stop.

Our emotions turn sour; our minds give us fear-based thoughts. We are swept back into the thought forms of the masses instead of our higher potential – our awakening Heart.

Music is here to remind us. Our minds can remember tunes and lyrics, but there's something about music that transcends the mind.

When the mind transcends itself, there are many possibilities. Not all of them good. At first, we hear a song and remember our first love or past times or our various created realities. As we blossom more, music allows us to access greater wholeness and greater love. Our awakening Hearts are our greater wholeness and our greater aliveness.

We then reach that point where we use music as carrier waves of our pure Heart Love. Even our own voices begin to carry greater Love, independent of what we are saying.

Chapter 5

THE THIRD DARK NIGHT

By the time I was a sophomore at Arroyo High, I had determined exactly what the rest of my life would be. I was to be a great musician! I would first go to a four-year college, obtain my teaching credential majoring in music. Upon graduating I would then join a famous rock group and hit the road. I would see the world, feel the crowds, have a lot of girlfriends who "understood" me, and solidify that place I once knew in my own back yard with Jing.

I knew it was going to happen. I practiced every day. I enrolled at California State University at Hayward. In the 1970s, CSUH was *the best* music college in California. I auditioned and got accepted to the "A" Jazz Band (there were two of them), the CS Jazz Jam Group, the Concert Band, and one of the CS Saxophone Chamber Quartets. I was also in the Jazz Band at Chabot College, a nearby community college. Each music major at Cal State had a private teacher for their instrument where we had to learn "crazy hard" pieces of music and perform recitals each semester in front of the entire music faculty who all sat there in the front row with clipboards. The audience included all my peers in the music department, including all the girls I had crushes on, and the other sax players – hoping for me to mess up so they could fill my spot in whatever group. It was intense but I loved it.

It was very competitive being a music major, purposely established that way to prepare us for the "real world" as musicians after graduation, *if* we made it that far. Less than half of the freshmen who started out as Cal State music majors actually completed the program.

At night and on weekends I was in a rock group called *Hot*

Ice. We played gigs mostly in the Bay Area. I was also taking private lessons from jazz bop master, Hal Stein, who had played with Charlie "Bird" Parker, Al Cohn, and other great musicians.

https://en.wikipedia.org/wiki/Hal_Stein

To master all the music, much of it memorized, my routine was to awake at 5:00AM and start practicing until my first classes started at 8:00AM. I was still living with my parents and they allowed me to section off a small "practice studio" in the garage, partially sound-proofed with a hundred or so egg cartons and thick rugs.

In the evening I practiced with *Hot Ice* and then more back home in the garage often until midnight or later. The one "break" in my playing schedule was watching Johnny Carson for thirty minutes with my mom and dad. I loved Johnny Carson, plus Doc Severinsen – Johnny's house band leader – had one of the greatest "Big Bands" around.

Most of the sax players at Cal State also took private lessons from Hal Stein. He was a great teacher and I learned from him most of my jazz skills, especially how to improvise on top of chord changes.

There was another sax teacher in town though, who unlike good-natured Hal, would not accept students unless they passed his audition. Only the best of the best could become his student. The word out was that he was ruthless and would shout and demand perfection.

Danny Pateris was his name. He had played with Dizzy Gillespie. That said it all. After two years with Hal, I decided to audition.

I drove to his house completely terrified of rejection or worse, making some stupid mistake and feeling the guillotine drop. Danny lived in South San Francisco in a Victorian house with a locked gate at the entrance. I had never encountered gates with intercoms where you would "buzz up" and they would "buzz you in." I saw the little button which I thought was a doorbell and pushed it. I didn't hear a ring, and a few seconds later I only stood there confused when I heard the buzz come back. "What the heck?" I thought. "I ring the doorbell and then the buzz sounds again?" What was I supposed to do? I just kept ringing back, until an angry Danny Pateris bolted out of the front door and yelled, "Push the damn gate open when you hear the buzz, asshole!"

"Sorry," I squeaked.

"What do you know how to play?"

"Saxophone," I answered.

"I know that man, I mean what pieces? Have you memorized any of Bird or Coltrane's solos? How about *Giant Steps*?"

I was regretting the whole idea of becoming one of his "special" students. My solar plexus was as tight as a clam.

"What kind of horn do you have?"

"A Selmer Mark VI," I replied.

"What's the serial number?"

I had never thought about the serial number of *anything* much less my prized Mark VI.

"I don't know..."

"It's about time you found out...it's important!" he barked.

He knew exactly where to look. It was a five-digit serial number starting with the number "5." He was happy.

"Okay, play anything for me, but face that wall, not me."

In those days, if you were a "hip" tenor player, you could not only play down-and-dirty rock n' roll sax like King Curtis, but also had to know Charlie Parker's fast bop licks, Coltrane's "inside" period of chordal mastery and the current hip sound which included the ability to reach super high notes, called altissimo. And, you had to play *fast.*

After about ninety seconds of playing all of the above into the wall, Danny shouted, "Shut the f**k up...stop playing *shit* in my home!!"

Holy crap, the guillotine had dropped. I was ready to go home with my tail between my legs.

"PLAY MIDDLE 'C' AS LONG AS YOU CAN," Danny then yelled.

Middle "C" was the first note you learn on a sax. Oh man, he was humiliating me. I played it...for as long as I could.

For the next fifty minutes of the lesson, that's all I played. Over and over again, middle "C" at various dynamics and lengths. Danny showed me how to breathe from my diaphragm and how to position my throat, embouchure and jaw muscles.

I played one note, the easiest note on the saxophone, for almost an hour.

"Bob, I want you to play one note per day for the next seven days. Tomorrow, start with "B," then "Bb," etc. By the time I see you again next week, you'll be on "G." It's all about *sound,* Bob. If you can play one note and move someone to tears, you've got it – but I ain't crying yet. It's time for you to open the gates, man!"

And then he said something I'll never forget.

"Your heart is good, Bob. That means you can become a great musician. Now you have to get your heart into everything you do, including your saxophone. Start each day doing a ten-minute meditation with your sax. It's a great horn, your

Selmer Mark VI - built at a time when the saxophone was chosen to be *the* horn to help lay rest the crazy war (World War II) and lift our pathetic heroism, shame, guilt, and horror out of our groins and into our hearts once again. I'm talking love and respect. Respect your horn, love your horn. When you play there should be no difference between your horn, your love, your respect and your heart. See you next Wednesday and this time push the fucking gate open when you hear the buzzer."

The next morning at 5:00AM, I held my sax in my arms like a mother with her newborn infant. Within a few seconds I saw the beings from the other worlds arrive. They would continue as my companions while I played everything from *Yakety Yak* by King Curtis, to the classical masterpiece, *Concertino de Camera* by Jacques Ibert, to...*Good Vibrations* by *The Beach Boys.*

https://www.youtube.com/watch?v=UJupHgof8iI

https://www.youtube.com/watch?v=-cHB3Rbz1OI

Toward the end of my first year at Cal State my jaw started to hurt. I was playing fourteen-plus hours per day and was completely obsessed with my music. Like any obsessed person at age nineteen, you simply ignore pain. By the beginning of my third year, the pain was constant and I could no longer pretend it wasn't there. Every time I would begin playing my sax my jaw would hurt so bad I had to take aspirin or ibuprofen just to keep playing.

Then one early morning in bed after a late gig my jaw began to hurt so bad I thought I was going to go crazy – but worse, I couldn't open my mouth! It was locked shut. What an absolutely horrible feeling. My whole body went into panic as I panted and hysterically tried ice packs and massage to get my mouth to open. I knew I had to calm down and somehow figure out how to relax my jaw muscles. After an hour of the slow diaphragmatic breathing that Danny had taught me, along with ice applied directly to both sides of my jaw, my mouth finally opened. I broke into an uncontrollable cry. "What the heck is going on now?" I thought.

I went to the Cal State Free Health Clinic on campus and the doctor on duty told me to see a dentist. I had worn braces in my early teens so I went to my orthodontist, who immediately said the pain was because I had too many teeth and that my wisdom teeth should immediately be removed. "Great!" I thought – this would solve my jaw spasms and constant pain. So my wisdom teeth were removed, all four of them at once. But after weeks of so-called recovery, my jaw still hurt.

I went to three more dentists with no advice until the third one suggested I see a newly founded clinic in Berkeley, called the *TMJ Clinic.*

TMJ stands for Temporomandibular Joint Disorders, which in the 1970s was a new thing for dentists to study and treat. It's a fancy term for all the muscles and intricate jaw bones together. I promptly got an appointment – Berkeley was only thirty minutes away – and they took x-rays of my jaw. In those days it took sometimes weeks before the results of x-rays were received by the dentists.

Even during the teeth extractions and massive pain, I continued to practice, play gigs, and met all my obligations in my various Cal State groups. *Advil* and ice were my constant companions.

After two full grueling weeks, they called me back to the Berkeley TMJ Clinic. Four dentists in white coats hoisted the x-rays onto the screen, switched on the massively bright light and began pointing at various parts of the negative.

"You've had an injury here – at the ball of your temporomandibular joint, Bob. It must have been when you were young, before the joints were fully grown."

"Yes, I crashed on my bike when I was eight or so, knocking myself unconscious and the doctor stitched my chin," I answered.

"That makes sense. You actually broke the bone here (pointing at a blob at the ball of the joint that meant nothing to me) and it didn't heal properly."

I was relieved. Finally, an explanation to all of this. "OK, what next...do you need to operate or something?" I innocently asked.

"There's no way to repair this, Bob. But, you don't have to! The problem is that when you play your saxophone, the position your embouchure takes puts a strain right at those muscles around the broken bone. That's what causes the pain and spasms. You'll just have to give up playing the sax, that's all. How about guitar – everyone is learning the guitar these days."

"Doctor, you don't understand, my saxophone is my *life*! I'm going to be a professional musician and then teach music until I die. Isn't there any operation or something you guys can do?" I implored.

"There's no operation for this Bob. You're young...you'll find another instrument."

In my diary I had kept track of almost everything I was experiencing in my life. I started making entries in the second grade and still write them to this day. My first "dark night" was the loss of Jing – or perhaps my innocence. My second "dark night" was the guilt I felt from the effects of my "mind power" over Linda Rodriguez. The experience of not being able to continue playing my saxophone was by far the "darkest night" I had experienced by age twenty.

I was in shock. I drove home in a trance. I actually played a gig that night with *Hot Ice*, faking my good-natured impromptus with the crowd at the club, since I was the band's MC (Master of Ceremonies). I had to joke with the crowd and encourage them to drink more. After I got home – it must have been 3:00AM – I wrote in my diary, "I must find something that can never be taken from me. I don't know what to do. I must find my Guru."

Chapter 6

THE GURU

I had read about gurus, Christian saints, Buddhists and American Indian shamans while growing up, and by the time I got to the eleventh grade, I was pretty much determined to find one at some point. I loved the concepts of Nirvana, Samadhi and Self-Realization. I loved the stories of Jesus and was even "saved" and "born-again" for a while not only because I wanted to see if it would bring me the peace and love I had experienced in my back yard with Jing, but because I wanted to see firsthand people overtaken by the Holy Spirit which I had read about. At one point during a rather intense Bible study, I found myself speaking in tongues. At least that's what everybody said it was. I was just out-of-my body via my emotional center – my throat Chakra. If any human activates their throat Chakra in this way, spontaneous sounds and words come out of the vocal chords. Often other 4D entities take charge for a while and use the body to speak, move, and even dance in ways the individual had no previous knowledge of. I learned more about all these phenomena later.

At that point though, I was in total despair. I thought of how Beethoven must have felt when he reached his most spectacular composition of the Ninth Symphony only to lose his hearing before the piece was ever performed. He was said to have died shaking his fist at God.

How could God have allowed this? All my years of practice, my dedication to others through my music and my years of meditating with my saxophone to become "one" with it. Now, I simply should start over with another instrument?

I began praying a simple prayer every morning and night, religiously. "God help me."

I went to the back yard to be with the nature spirits I had grown up with, but they couldn't care less about my TMJ or my career ambitions.

I longed for Jing. Maybe he could show me some magic, some natural healing remedy. I prayed directly to him, to God the Father, Jesus, Gautama Buddha, Mother Mary and Quan Yin. No one showed up and there were no answers or revelations.

Cal State is on a hill and during the winter months the entire campus is wrapped in fog, especially at night. I loved the spookiness of it and since I would often stay late in one of the practice rooms in the music building, I would relish the cool evening fog air when I finally left to descend down the hill.

One particular night was exceptionally foggy and it took me a long time to remember where I had parked so many hours earlier that morning. When I found my car I noticed something on the windshield. A ticket! I had parked in a red zone. Since Cal State had its own police, the tickets were settled right at the campus police station, open twenty-four hours a day.

I decided to pay the ticket that night; it only made sense since "everything was wrong and worthless with my life." I was twenty-two and my thoughts were often suicidal. When I turned thirteen my father made a big deal to tell my sister and me that he kept his 22 Magnum WMR pistol hidden in the closet, loaded. He then took my sister and me out to the fields to teach us how to shoot it. It scared the heck out of me and I tried to forget about his disclosure and combat education. Nine years later and after concluding that there was no further reason for me to live, I went to the closet. I carefully took the gun out of the metal bullet-proof box and pointed it at my head with my finger on the trigger. My hand started shaking so badly and my heart was beating so fast that I knew I couldn't go through with it. It was a turning point perhaps, but for me at the time it was only a dramatization of my own self-pity.

What changed my life forever was not the confrontation with my father's guns, but the confrontation with a silly parking ticket and my odd encounter with the Campus Police.

There was a happy-go-lucky "Officer O'Brian" type of officer, alone at his desk inside the Campus Police facility...a red-faced Irish looking man with a smile that seem to extend off his face. He perked me up.

"Don't worry lad, we all make mistakes! I'll find your file and take off this ticket right away. You got $2?" I had the two bucks and was ready to pay my debt to Cal State.

There was something that inexplicably grabbed my attention on Officer O'Brian's desk. A photo frame with the back toward me. For some reason, I couldn't stop looking at it. I assumed it was of his wife or kids or both; maybe his dog was in the photo too. Why was I magnetized to it? Why was I compelled to walk around to his side of the desk to see who was in it? I struggled; I couldn't remember if it was bad manners to walk around somebody's desk to look at their photos, but I had to see it. O'Brian was in another room so I quickly walked around and quite unexpectedly, saw my Guru.

It was a photo of Maharishi Mahesh Yogi who brought Transcendental Meditation (TM) to the world. I had heard of him before and even seen his picture on occasion, but there was something very different about that night at Officer O'Brian's desk. There was a gold aura literally coming out of the photo. Maharishi's eyes seemed alive; my Heart felt a wonderful love.

"Is this The Maharishi?" I ask timidly when Officer O'Brian returned.

"Oh yes! I've been meditating for almost a year and it has changed my life." He proceeded to tell me all about how he had met Maharishi and delighted in telling me every detail. The only thing I could do was stare at the picture. I barely heard or saw anything else. I knew Maharishi was an answer to my prayers.

"You ought to go to a TM intro lecture this coming Wednesday night. They're having one at Meiklejohn Hall at 7:00PM."

"I will be there!" I said.

I went to the intro lecture and the following Saturday paid $50, received my mantra, and learned Transcendental Meditation. I was, as meditators later used to say, *blissed out*.

I obtained a copy and devoured Maharishi's book, *The Art of Living and the Science of Being*." It all made perfect sense. He presented all aspects of living as an art, and all aspects of spirituality or "Being" as a science..."science" meaning repeatable, verifiable and measurable. "Art" meaning creative, spontaneous and within structure.

I took Maharishi's course called *The Science of Creative Intelligence*, at the local TM Center. Later that year I enrolled to attend *Maharishi International University* in, of all places, Iowa. MIU was, at the time, a fully accredited international university – with a number of B.S. and B.A. degrees offered.

One of the things I loved about Maharishi's teachings was that desires were not meant to be denied. They were meant to be fulfilled. Fulfilling desire was part of the "art" of life. "Being," he said, or "bliss consciousness" was our birthright. It was "The Self" eternal, unbounded and always free.

Jesus said, "Seek ye first the kingdom of heaven, and all else will come to you." To Maharishi this meant, "Find the kingdom as 'love-bliss,' our true Self, the very Oneness of everyone." The more "Being" was established and eventually lived constantly, then the "Art" of life, the fulfillment of all desires, becomes effortless.

How was I to fulfill my desire to be a musician I thought? One thing that Maharishi said was that as you expand your consciousness, desires get fulfilled in different ways. I thought what he said was either a cop-out or something I needed to experience. He also said, "Knowledge (or reality) is different in different states of Consciousness. Your reality is very different when you are in dream consciousness, right? And, even different still in deep sleep. Waking state is a blanket term for only one of many states of consciousness when you are awake. What you perceive and how you perceive it will automatically change as your consciousness changes."

I was fine not to worry about my music at that point, and I almost didn't bring my saxophone with me as I took a fifty-hour *Greyhound* bus ride into the coldest winter ever recorded in the history of Iowa, the winter of 1977. I arrived at MIU on January 6th and just in time for new student orientation on Friday, January 7th. I wrote in my diary that night, "I feel like I've arrived home."

I loved every bit of it. The dress code – we had to wear a sport coat or suit and tie every day to classes – the strict military style discipline (each minute you were late for class you were docked a point off your grade), and most of all, the fact that all students and faculty practiced TM twice a day. My parents were terrified I had joined a cult, but I called them once a week to assure them I was okay, and even sent pictures of my text books which included quantum physics, calculus, biology and English lessons.

The music department was, of all places, beneath the library building. After a week or so, I took the leap and went there, pulled out my sax, and started blowing – just for fun – in one of the practice rooms. Within minutes there was a knock at the door, and I met John Wubbenhorst, who remains one of my closest friends to this day.

"Man, you're good! I have just formed a jazz fusion group

here and I want you to join us! Please come tomorrow night to Room 24 for our practice. I've got charts written out and everything; you'll be perfect for us."

The next night I was amazed as *The Welcome Band* played through difficult charts in the style of Chick Corea and *Weather Report*. Most of the compositions were originals John had written. He played flute and piano and was damn good. *The Welcome Band* members consisted of drums, congas, base, guitar, piano, a jazz female singer, John on flute and me on sax. Before each practice, we meditated for five minutes. There was something different I spotted, even before MIU, in meditators...a kind of sky-blue around their Heart Chakras. Chakras are, of course, the centers of spiritual power within our bodies.

"With Bob, *The Welcome Band* is complete! Our first concert will be Saturday April 16th at the theatre," John announced.

I was able to play my sax for up to three hours before my jaw started to spasm, but that was more than enough time for *The Welcome Band*.

In February we were told by Dennis Raimondi, Dean of Students, that Paul Horn was coming to MIU to give a free concert to the student body in March. Paul Horn! Wow! He was famous back then as he had almost single-handedly started the New Age recording industry with his *Inside The Taj Mahal* album, which went platinum.

When Paul arrived on campus a few days before his scheduled concert, Dennis introduced *The Welcome Band* to him. He asked if we would play a few numbers for him. We did and afterwards he came up to John and me and asked, "I'd like you both, your drummer and your bass player to open our concert with me. Do you think the others in your band will be offended?"

"No! They'll be blissed out to hear that we're going to play with you! There's no competition here," we assured him.

So, with one rehearsal, I was on stage playing with the great Paul Horn.

My great musical moments were yet to come however. First, *The Welcome Band* concert in April. There was a song that John wrote called, *Creation*, which featured Robin on cello and me on sax. It was almost entirely improvised with this simple theme – *from nothingness to something-ness.*

The theatre was packed and the first two numbers we played were flawless. Then came *Creation*.

My eyes were closed; I remembered Danny's instructions to be "one with my horn." I started off with a long lingering low sub-tone, only possible from my years of diaphragmatic breathing. The rest wasn't me at all. The horn played itself, just like Danny said it would.

I had put my Sony cassette recorder at the side of the stage, with a blank 120-minute tape, and pressed record before the concert began. That recording would serve as yet another turning point in my life.

https://www.youtube.com/watch?v=1mOD2pudjD0

Chapter 7

GOOD VIBRATIONS

My second semester at MIU was a bit different. John Wubbenhorst and most of the members of *The Welcome Band* had left. On the up side, there were three awesome jazz musicians straight from the Berklee College of Music – arguably the top private jazz college in the country. Instead of *The Welcome Band* with eight members, now I was playing pure jazz standards in a traditional jazz quartet. And these guys were pros! Yet another desire fulfilled!

There was always construction going on at MIU – old buildings being torn down, and new ones put up. When one of the faculty housing facilities way out past the unused football field was under renovation, the word spread fast across the student body. The entire building, the equivalent of a small house, was being changed into a recording studio! A what? The rumors spread even more quickly when it was thought that the recording studio was being built for none other than *The Beach Boys*.

Like all of us, I thought that would be so cool if it were true. We all knew that *The Beach Boys* had learned TM from Maharishi in India on the same courses *The Beatles*, Donovan, Paul Horn, and other celebrities were on. Like George from *The Beatles*, Mike from *The Beach Boys* stayed meditating and became a supporter of both Maharishi and his technique of meditation.

But a recording studio for *The Beach Boys* in the middle of Iowa? Really? I thought it was going a bit too far.

One day while checking my mail there was an envelope with my name on it – but it hadn't been mailed (all students picked

44

up their mail in the Student Hall in alphabetized boxes). Someone on campus had obviously put it in my box.

Dear Bob Williams,

I heard you play sax last semester with The Welcome Band. Do you have a recording of it? If so, please find me at the cafeteria tonight in the Southeast corner. I'm part of campus construction.

Jai Guru Dev, Scott Jamilson

I brought my Sony and met Scott that night exactly as he had instructed. A bunch of my friends who I usually ate with followed me.

"Hi Bob," Scott said to me nervously. "Let's go outside." My friends looked offended but didn't follow us.

Once outside, Scott told me that indeed *The Beach Boys* were building a studio out at the faculty house farthest west, and once completed they would be recording an album there. Scott had heard the sound engineers talking about flying out a horn section from Los Angeles when one of them said he had heard there was a "really good" sax player right here at MIU on campus.

"How good?" they asked.

"Well, I think I can get a tape from the group he was in last semester. And, he also played with Paul Horn," Scott told them.

"Try to get the tape, but don't let it out to anyone else that *The Beach Boys* are coming. We've been told to keep it on the 'QT' so as to not distract the students."

I gave Scott the 120-minute cassette; he made me promise not to tell anyone, and said that he would contact me via my mailbox if they were interested in using me.

Mike Love of *The Beach Boys* made the final decision, and a month later I was overdubbing horn parts with three other guys flown in from L.A. – over and over again until we got it just right. What was completely awesome was hearing many of *The Beach Boys'* vocal harmonies which had already been recorded, and that we were superimposing our horns' lines upon.

Those *Beach Boys'* vocal harmonies! For a moment I was back in my garage in 1966 listening to *Good Vibrations* for the first time. No one could sound like *The Beach Boys* with their vocal harmonies.

One evening I bravely took a hike to the recording studio after normal hours. The doors were open and I heard some of the tracks being played over and over. I walked in, and there was Mike Love, sitting alone at the controls, both listening and making notes.

"Hey Bob!" he said like we were old friends.

"Hi Mike. Hey, I was wondering if I could go on the road with you guys after the album is done?"

"We're not touring too much these days Bob, but I'm starting a production company in Santa Barbara. Do you have any other skills?"

"You bet, Mike, I worked as a part-time bookkeeper back at Cal State."

"What about your studies here at MIU?"

"I'm out of money. Once this semester is over, I'm out until I can afford to get back in."

I never got back in. By the spring of 1978 I was working full time for *LoveSongs Productions* in a large beautiful estate, "The Love Estate" in Santa Barbara, California, owned by Mike Love. It was fourteen two-story houses plus a beautiful production office overlooking the mesa, not to mention Mike's personal home, literally on a massive cliff overlooking the ocean. I lived in one of the houses with two of our twenty-seven employees.

Were all my desires really manifesting as Maharishi had said?

Whenever *The Beach Boys* performed over the next three years, I was able to play sax in the horn section. My favorite song, now on stage with Brian Wilson and *The Beach Boys* and thousands of fans – *Good Vibrations*.

Chapter 8
LIGHT

I had continued to get weaker, thinner and more desperate. I was now down to 110 lbs. At six-foot-three, I looked like a holocaust victim. Although I was still working for the production company owned by Mike Love and *The Beach Boys*, my work activities grew less and less. I simply could not get up and down the stairs.

The local doctors grew more perplexed, having little clue as to how I had descended to such a decrepit state. Because I had been a musician I must have done a lot of drugs which had toxified my liver, they thought. It wasn't true. I never did any drugs. I smoked marijuana a few times when I was a teenager, but nothing since then. Marijuana made me far too spacey and disoriented. Since I was never quite in my body anyway, disorientation was the last thing I needed. Truthfully, I was terrified of drugs, because of what I had seen in the auras of those who had become addicted and even those who were just trying them out. I also didn't drink alcohol because every time I did I got horribly sick, not to mention the rampant alcoholism in my family on both sides.

The Santa Barbara medical doctors knew only that there was something terribly wrong. I would see them about once every two weeks. I would look worse each time and the blood chem-panels only said that something bad was happening to my body, but not *what* was happening.

The first official diagnosis was liver failure, then hepatitis, then kidney disease and then unknown viruses.

"If you keep going the way you're going, you'll be dead in six months," I was warned.

"You must admit yourself to the hospital so we can monitor you twenty-four hours a day and figure out what is really going on! We should put you on an IV drip to keep you from losing any more weight – to keep you alive."

"Admit yourself to the hospital now!"

I went back home wondering about this. I woke up in the middle of the night. I knew that if I were to die, going to the hospital would only speed things up.

> When you are confronted with difficult decisions that you know will have major consequences, there are specific Universal Laws of the Heart which are seeking you.
>
> The first sign that you are approaching the Laws of the Heart is <u>confusion</u>. When you are <u>not</u> confused, you are either listening primarily to your mind or you are completely in the present moment of radical aliveness. For most of us on Earth at this time, it is the former.
>
> When you become confused during major confrontations in life, do not try to figure things out by thinking, pondering and analyzing. Accept confusion. Be okay with confusion. A secret doorway will open up, not by will or mind, but because of your acceptance.
>
> The doorway opens when you least expect it. This is the Law during this time of Earth.
>
> The Law is Love, Devotion and Surrender.
>
> 1. Love means totally and absolutely accepting everything exactly as it is right now.
>
> 2. Devotion means turning everything over that you have accepted, to whatever it is that you know to be greater than your mind, body and emotions...greater than any thought, sensation or feeling...greater than your consciousness at that moment.

3. *Surrender to that greater potential. If you are not sure what that greater power is, that means you're following the Law. Surrender is not resisting anything. It is the ultimate "letting go." You are willing to go with any decision without concern. Surrender also doesn't mean pushing something away with effort, or holding onto a concept of God (or a greater power) with intent. When you truly surrender, you'll know it. Everything just lets go on its own. The confusion becomes total confusion without concern; the pain becomes total pain without resistance; your love becomes total love without conditions.*

That night, I consciously chose to stop all my efforts to heal... all my trying to find out what was wrong with me...trying to find some way to feel better. I simply surrendered into my tiredness and weakness.

At first it took several days of simply getting up, working, and doing the basics in life. My habit of thinking "Maybe this will help me, maybe if I saw this type of doctor or healer..." was there, but I soon got used to not trying. I didn't stop what I felt was helping me. I continued to take vitamins, do simple yoga and eat good food. But, I wasn't seeking health anymore. After a while in fact, I wasn't seeking anything.

About a month later, I could barely walk. My friends were aghast, almost begging me to go to the hospital.

I refused.

One morning I woke up feeling like I was going to vomit. I stumbled to the bathroom but instead of vomiting, I fell to the floor unconscious...perhaps a couple of seconds passed where I was above my body seeing it lifeless on the bathroom floor. I was either dying or dead. Then nothing, absolutely nothing.

Instead of waking up in my body or around my body like the previous times, something happened which can only be described by me, now, writing this book for you, for us, is *remembering*. What happened was not "something happening to me." It was not happening at all.

The only word I can find to describe it is Light.

There was/is ONLY Light.

I

WE

YOU

ALL IS LIGHT

There was no separate body or form of any kind associated with this Light. There was nobody looking at this Light, searching for The Light, or running away from The Light. There was ONLY Light. There was no separate one reflecting upon The Light. There was no time, space and no difference of any kind. There was no one to "realize" The Light. The Light is Completion. The Light has no beginning or end. The Light is full.

There were no emotions in this Light, no different feelings and no contrasts of any kind. There was no body, no mind, no feeling or emotion. There was no "relationship" to The Light.

Then...subtle differences. Differences mean movement. Subtle movement.

SOUND.

And then, there "I" was.

"I" became, again.

At first the functioning "I" was noticing these subtle almost unperceivable movements "as" Light. "I" was all of it. Not the "I" previously identified with "Robert Odus Williams" and all the memories and stories associated with that identity. Just a pure singularity noticing movement in itself, as itself, and from itself.

At that point the Light *was* a flickering, shimmering brightness. There was some dualistic relationship within The Light. The Light was flickering...and there was an "*I*" observing and aware of the flickering.

At this point there was still no "Robert" or anything other than the flickering. Flickering this way and that. "This way" was therefore in contrast to "that way."

And then suddenly, there "I" was "looking" at this brilliance. The identity associated with my life on earth rebirthed itself and filled my awareness. My "mind" was back. I was gently and lovingly reconnected to "my" personality and body.

> *Words will never convey the Truth of Light. Words will, therefore, never convey the Truth of You.*
>
> *It's okay. Enjoy your mind's attempts – with words, images and concepts. Music, art and poetry. These are gifts for your explorations. Ah-ha moments, revelations.*
>
> *You are all destined to wake up, as if from a deep dream. You will become awake to the truth that anything your mind has stored, projected, thought of, or imagined is but a mere drop within the Infinite Ocean of who you are.*
>
> *This doesn't mean the drops are insignificant. In fact, it is only through these drops that you, as humans, can become aware of the ocean.*
>
> *You are the Ocean of Light and Truth.*

You are Love. You are not less than Love, nor are you limited by your current thoughts of Love right now. A thought is a contraction of Love – useful at times, particularly now during this current time of Earth.

Earth is amazingly unique. It is an especially beautiful place within the entire Cosmos.

You are very fortunate to have been chosen to experience the earth at this time.

This is indeed, the time for understanding one of the most massive polarities in the Universe.

Pain, despair, cruelty, trauma and suffering – along with true ecstasy, beauty, creativity, aliveness and...paradise.

I was Shimmering Light and Sound.

Three things:

> I, the subject
>
> Light and Sound, or the object
>
> And the mechanism of the subject/object relationship – the bridge between.
>
> I, the Lover
>
> You, the Beloved
>
> The Heart, the process of Loving

Complete differences – a subject experiencing a different object – alive with complete oneness – the subject and object being no different – is now being called "Living Love from the Heart." The more Whole the Heart is, the more the differences are seen and appreciated and the more oneness and unity is real.

The fully alive conjunction of Unity in Diversity, which will and must manifest as paradise, is the intention of planet Earth, starting with the first photon from the infinite, ending with the largest physical manifestation – Universes upon Universes dissolving into Infinity.

A grand intention.

As I perceived the brilliant Light, I simultaneously felt both a pulling force toward it (collapsing the three: me, the light and the process) along with a pulling force away from it (into more of the "me," the manifestations of the light and the process of perceptions).

Then I felt my first emotion – a longing to be One with The Light, and a resolve to be apart from it.

Conflict.

What happened next made the experience perfect.

A Being appeared between The Light and me. Such a beautiful Being. A brilliant gold form, semi-translucent but alive with pure, untethered, vast and incomparable Love.

Oh my God! I was not only experiencing this Love, I knew at that point that I had indeed come from it. No! I was it and it was me at the same time. The Paradox of paradoxes... resolved and complete in the reality of Oneness...the Heart of all of us!

For an eternity without concern, without any discomfort or longing, without any desire or want, this paradox continued.

And then there was a kind of weight within the "me" part, creating even more contrast, even more paradox of difference.

I remembered that I was, or had been, "Robert."

I remembered my body. For a reason I'll never fully under-stand, I felt compelled to turn away from The Light, as difficult as it was. I saw my body again on the bathroom floor.

An understanding upon returning to my body was that the mechanism of perception is not confined to a body's nervous system. Which "eye" was seeing the body on the floor with closed eyes? Those answers would come later, from more specific and distinct journeys throughout the inter-dimensional worlds.

But for now it didn't matter. I knew that my physical body on the floor was dead or close to it, and that "I," was now more alive than I could have possibly imagined.

I turned back to the Being.

"I want to return to The Light," I said.

"It is your choice."

I was stunned at this response. How could I choose anything other than this unified *bliss*, this unending ecstasy without pain, suffering or any need of any kind? And I knew, that we were *all* – all those I loved dearly – all humans in fact, were alive, free and fulfilled within as part of and completely as The Light. What kind of a choice is this?

"Is there a purpose for me to go back?" I asked.

"Yes."

"Is it those that have yet to remember The Light, the Bliss? My mother, father, sister and Lisa?"

"Much more."

I didn't have to answer. I knew I had to return.

I began to "descend." I first saw such wondrous sights impos-sible to fully describe. They were Beings because they radiated such Love, Compassion and an All-Knowing-ness of all things, including our great struggles here on Earth. Whenever I experience True, Pure, and Real Unconditional Love here on Earth, I remember these Beings. These Great Beings embodied spherical forms...Love in Motion...orbs of such Purpose and Love.

I was not destined to stay there, however.

The next level was as if completely full of endless symbols, patterns, geometries and mandalas. Such beautiful mandalas! Happening simultaneous to the mandalas were the most incredible sounds I have ever heard – sizzling, blissful and euphoric.

The next were The Archangels (as I was later able to identify them). Each of them with vast "bodies," distinct yet all so full of Love and the purest compassion and empathy possible – each with a distinct vibration and therefore, a distinct form.

The next level I saw more human-like forms. I would discover these great ones to be what are now referred to as The Ascended Masters. Ones that had incarnated on Earth, but had ascended to a grand level of service to us all. I also recognized at this level Jesus, Mary, Buddha and many others. All seemed to pause their grand duties to acknowledge my brief presence in their world. My body at this point, was not defined except within that subject, object and process of relationship reality.

The next level "down" is full of loving beings of all kinds and shapes. Angels and guides live here. I would come to know them very well in the years to follow. I spent a bit more time here as they seemed to recognize me, but soon bid me farewell.

The next level contained humans who were in transition after just leaving their bodies on Earth and those who are preparing for their incarnation. In other words, what most of us here on Earth call birth and death. They were accompanied by great angelic beings along with their individual angel guides and celestial companions.

Next "down" was a sad sight. This is what I later identified as the lower fourth dimension where humans are caught "in between." This is a state where the person was either killed suddenly and was not at all aware of the quick transition or, the person was so attached to Earth, loved ones, and/or their body, that when the death process began, it could not fully complete.

> Since The Light is always everywhere present, it can be totally or partially perceived at any time by any form of consciousness.
>
> When a human soul experiences the pulling away of the singular identification with their physical body, at the time of death of the physical body, previously positioned veils are removed as per Cosmic Law.
>
> Once a person's contracted identities are out-shined by The Light, then any unresolved thoughts, words or actions position themselves vibrationally into their next highest level of existence, their next "body" associated with these energies, also according to Cosmic Law.
>
> If a personality's individual Will is too attached to the previous incarnation, then there is a great slowing down of the evolutionary process. Also, if a person's death is so sudden that The Light is not able to be perceived in place of the one's actions at the time of his or her sudden death, then those actions and environmental realities at the time of death continue on, but at a much slower rate.
>
> The fourth dimension is still under the influence of the speed of light, but because photons are tremendously faster at this

level, the relative time compared to the 3D plane is much slower. One day in this 4D domain could be many thousands of years in the 3D domain.

There are several levels to this stagnate state. At the higher vibratory levels are souls who are simply living their apparent earthly lives in mundane manners, but because they are not connected to the circadian rhythms and cycles of the solar system (the physical laws of photon light, etc.), they have no concept of time. They are stuck but relatively content.

The lower levels contain ones who have turned away from The Light because of their unwillingness to accept forgiveness of themselves.

Forgiveness is not discriminatory, it is a Law and any being is forgiven for any action at any point of surrendering to The Light, or to God in any form or shape they believe in.

This doesn't mean that horrible actions are condoned, quite the contrary. It means that the ignorance of our Unity which all individuals will have been or will be confronted with, is forgiven. Any action which separates or causes pain of any part of the Universe is simply because of the temporary ignorance of our Oneness.

Accepting or giving forgiveness allows, by Law, more Light to become active in the individual consciousness including their bodies, minds and spiritual identities. This is why we feel in various ways, "realized," "born again," "saved," "healed," or "set free." All of these qualities are inherent in the Unity of Light and Sound.

For the souls residing at ease levels of 4D, there is by Grace, a plan. The Light will soon become so bright that their attachments will release and they will quickly find their next highest level of good. Their contractions and turning away *will literally be outshined by Grace.*

No one will be left behind.

Chapter 9

PARADISE

Then there was peace. Complete blissful, alive peace. I began to feel my own body again. In rapid succession, I felt a place at the center of my forehead, then my lungs (which were now breathing), then my sexual and eliminatory organs, then my knees, my feet, and finally my own beating heart.

I was alive – in "my" body again. My eyes were still closed but I remember hearing the most beautiful sounds I had ever heard on Earth – with my now awakened physical sensory ears!

This was not the celestial music of the higher dimensions; these were actual physical sounds vibrating my eardrums! I heard the sounds of the garden outside where I lived in Santa Barbara, California, the sound of the ocean and birds singing. I had never heard conventional sounds in this way before, so divinely beautiful.

I understood at once, a complete knowingness:

> *Earth was intended to be a paradise.*

> *Earth has the blueprint to be a place without suffering and cruelty.*

> *Earth has the codes and informational templates to awaken us completely.*

I stood up with my eyes fully open. I was alive!

I looked outside my window for several minutes, still in awe.

I went to my bedroom and wrote down as many things as I could remember from the event that changed my life.

I gave my notice at *LoveSongs Productions*, leaving the entertainment business, *The Beach Boys*, and other celebrities I worked with such as John Travolta and Charles Lloyd. From my savings, which was huge to me at that point, I became a 33% owner in *Spruton Sprouting Company* in Flinn Springs, California, two hours east of San Diego. To our knowledge, Spruton was the first completely organic sprouting company in the US supplying commercial outlets – mostly health foods stores and Chinese restaurants.

On the property there was a Quonset hut – just like the ones my father had told me about in the war – with two rows of trays which grew all kinds of sprouts. My house was on the property and it was there that I embarked on journeys more interesting than any that I had ever taken before, and I can truthfully say, have ever had since then.

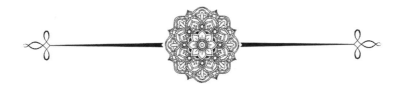

Chapter 10
ALIVE IN OTHER WORLDS

Since I had been meditating for about four years by then, I was no foreigner to "The Absolute" or complete silence and peace within. A month had passed since "The Event" in Santa Barbara.

After about ten minutes into meditation, the pure dazzling unmistakable Light began showing itself. Out of the silence and the nothingness it came. It came closer and closer, filling the "darkness" of nothingness – The Absolute – with Light, brighter and brighter.

I remained a witness to the increasing brightness until suddenly, my experience turned to complete and utter fear. A tightness gripped my solar plexus. My breathing went from an almost unperceivable rate to panting.

Then I remembered what I had done just a month earlier.

> *To cross any gap, any chasm, any blockage toward higher states of Truth and Aliveness, you must completely and utterly accept what is...in this present moment AND...completely and utterly surrender to that which you are resisting.*

> *At certain times in our own growth and evolution, you must allow that which you resist to overtake you completely. You Love it unconditionally.*

> *At first, "It" - whatever it is – your fear of some kind in whatever form – will increase. It will trigger emotions.*

> *Keep being with them. Keep surrendering to them. If you cry, cry. If you shout, shout. Make no intention or effort to alter them in any way.*

Then, by order of Universal Law your mental body will trigger. All kinds of thoughts and commentaries on the experience will be presented to you. "You should get up; you should stop this process; you should breathe..." For any thought that comes, you continue to accept, surrender to them and Love unconditionally.

Again by Law, your body will resist your total surrender. It will resist because indeed it is programmed to resist danger and death. Your mind is responsible for the life, no matter how short or long, of your current mortal body. It pulls up all the files from the time of your birth and before, to survive, grow and thrive...to stay breathing, alive, and with as much comfort, consolation and safety as possible.

You keep loving, surrendering. The mind's role is no longer needed at this level. You accept it fully. By law, it recedes and finally is released.

It is also fine to have hopes, dreams and desires. You do not destroy them. You love them in the same way – without any motive or agenda to hold on to them.

You surrender everything to that which is greater than yourself, to God, to your Guru, to Nothing if that is all there is ultimately. You surrender your life and anything associated with it.

More and more they will all increase perhaps – the thoughts, emotions, body sensations, pain, coughing, gasping and then experiences of ecstasy, bliss and great happiness. Those are still "on the side you are on."

Keep going further in.

Keep surrendering – completely accepting – completely allowing – anything and everything that you are, everything that you are aware of, your past, your future and your desires.

Your attention is most alive when it accepts and even cherishes that which you resist the most. They are portals.

I was completely willing to die. I knew death was only a transition from one state to another. I had awakened in the Light with utter and complete faith, and to the paradox of faith toward an outcome while completely with the willingness for nothing to ever happen again. The acceptance of complete loss and failure of any previous motive or temporary achievement, understanding, realization and contentment.

By Law – by Grace, as has been in every case since then, I awoke.

But this time, I awoke in the reality of symbols – the same as when I was "returning" to my body in Santa Barbara...beautiful amazing symbols, mandalas and sacred geometries.

Ah, and then as before, I became aware of the three things again.

> *The experience.*

> *The experiencer.*

> *The process of experiencing.*

I surrendered once again to the same process, locating that which was the reality I most resisted (returning to the physical plane) and accepting it completely.

I awakened this time in the reality of the Great Masters of Light.

As I was experiencing the Light of the Great Masters, I let "this" too be gone for something greater...each time a "dying" even more. And then I would "wake up" in one of the domains I described earlier. Full of information, technical know-how and Grace.

Ultimately, as I continued this dying process, I reached a point where I became completely unconscious. I had no awareness whatsoever...for up to about twenty minutes according to my clock back home at Flinn Springs.

I coughed, sputtered and flayed a bit. And then there I was again, sitting in the lotus position on my meditation couch.

Like a vivid dream, I remembered where I had been. I wrote everything I could remember in my journals. The symbols, the sacred geometries and the information.

This process continued almost every day for twenty-seven months.

There was a resonance with this process that I knew had something to do with our purpose and our time on Earth together. Little did I know this would form the basis of the 108 Quantum Code Technology.

I continued daily.

To help ground myself, I obtained a photo of the Master I saw just this side of the complete Light before returning to my body in Santa Barbara.

He was my reference for reincarnation, not into a new body, but into the same body which was born to me in 1954. The "blue baby body" which had grown in so many different ways, been poisoned, suffered greatly and eventually morphed into the one on the meditation couch.

He was also my reference for Love, Devotion and Surrender. "To Him, for Him, from Him" or "to Her, for Her, from Her" helps the mind offer up. It allows the Heart to eventually take over and to lead us to where our minds, motives, desires and agendas could not.

Although my body was also part of the great Light, it was

as a mere drop of water compared to the ocean of vastness and completeness...previously, always and forever morphing, adjusting and moving.

> *The body – the earth – all physical reality – is always chang-ing and moving. Some movements take trillions of years. Some movements take a trillionth of a millisecond...outward, inward, vast and small.*
>
> *Pure Consciousness never changes, never moves, never gets involved.*
>
> *Pure consciousness becoming conscious OF ITSELF, is the first step in the awakening of all of us on this dear planet.*

I lived this all the time in Flinn Springs.

Then I had an idea.

Could "I" affect the growth, health and overall quality of the sprouts in my farm?

It was my first scientific experiment.

I went to the Quonset hut at 4:00AM one morning, well before any of our work crew arrived.

Chapter 11

EMOTIONS

After I began my intensive study of emotions as they correspond to each of our seven primary Chakras, I created a chart. To enter the secrets of my own Heart, I would first identify what I was feeling and what I was thinking. My emotions became doorways into my own soul, and then into various "soul groups" currently incarnated at this time...and finally to the One Heart, the One Love of the entire human race.

These Emotional States are:

Egotism	Conceit
Narcissism	Over-Aggressiveness
Balance	Courage and Confidence
Strength	Attachment
Overenthusiasm	Denial
Addiction to Pleasurable Things	Anger Toward Others
Frustration	Rage and Hatred
Attachment to Things and Concepts	Fanaticism
Co-dependency	Sympathy
Pity for Others	Fixation on Negativity
Grief and Sadness	Self-Pity and Despair
Victimization	Disappointment
Emptiness	Fear

Terrors

Emptiness

Pain

Addiction to Harmful Things

Guilt

Anxiety and Confusion

Jealousy

Comfort and Evenness

Humility

Disappointment

Aversion

Denial

Anger Toward Self

Depression

Selfishness

Resentment

Warmth and Compassion

Conditional Love

Chapter 12

THE LOWER WORLDS

The screeching sounds became almost unbearable. Where was I and why? I had started my journey from such a beautiful place, seeing elves, wizards and colorful beings of all shapes and sizes. I was so grateful to have been invited to visit such a world.

But the sounds, at first almost unperceivable, had grown with such horrible dissonance that my ears began throbbing with pain, my body felt like it would break apart from the magnitude of the discordant oscillations.

We are a multitude of bodies. Our most obvious is our physical one. Our current incarnation, the one that is reading these words right now, associate with the physical, mental, and emotional experiences we've had since birth, all the pleasures and pains, and the countless chemical changes and the actual changes this body has gone through.

We have many more bodies we use. The one most of us can remember are the bodies we use to experience our nightly dreams. There are also other ones we use when we "travel" either between sleeping and dreaming, or with what are called "out of body" experiences.

Depending upon the dimensional type and function of these bodies, our "Metaselves" govern the nature of our sensational experience.

The body I had assumed during my journey below the surface of the earth was one of those in which I still had access to the five senses.

Had something gone terribly wrong? Did the tall wizard-like

man, complete with the long grey beard and pointed hat, forget his promise to lead me to a "magical land of crystals and wonders...?"

I fell upon my hands and knees crying out, "I CANNOT TAKE THIS ANYMORE!!" The horrible sounds, massive now, were causing my body to tremble uncontrollably.

I blacked out. Again I was nothing; there was nothing...no heartbeat, no breath.

Like a baby whose mother had temporarily become distracted only to return to find her child dangling dangerously from a swing set almost to be strangled, I was at once held again.

The sounds completely ceased. My body, mind and emotions were comforted. I'm not sure who "held" me but the degree of comfort and love was unmistakable. I was so thankful.

I looked up and my eyes began to adjust to a most peaceful yet powerful sight. It was a giant three-dimensional symbol formed by what looked to be enormous beams of coherent and colored light.

Each beam was hovering as the light-sabers did in *Star Wars*, except that each was an indescribably different color. These were no ordinary colors. Although they had the qualities I had seen on the surface of the earth, these were formed by a magnificent combination of both solid matter and celestial lumina.

I gazed upon this structure for what seemed like hours (although in these realms, the position of the sun, and therefore the human definition of time, were irrelevant).

I then began to see beyond the giant light symbol, between the brilliant and radiant beams. On the other side I began to see a lake of the most sublime nature. It was reflecting no stars or moon above, but the brilliance from what looked to be huge quartz crystals around the perimeter.

I then saw the familiar swirling beings that I had seen over and over again in the back yard while growing up. Much smaller and stationary than Jing of course, but with a shimmering that reminded me of how long it had been since his sudden departure. I wished he was here with me now.

My reminiscing stopped as I saw what appeared to be...what was it? I squinted and strained to see, only to find that the more I tried, the less I saw.

I remembered once again...the Law.

I released any effort. The more I released and let go of any desire, journey, want, and curiosity, the more clear the structure became.

The wizard Merlin was now on the other side of the lake, between the pyramid and the shore, calling me forth. How was I to get past the light symbol? When I approached it closer, the beam fields blocked me and even knocked me back as I tried to push my way through.

Yet Merlin kept signaling me to come, expecting me to get past the light beams AND to get all the way across the lake!

> *The Laws are the laws. They can be violated, but only with effort, energy and consequences.*
>
> *Best to learn The Laws and abide by them.*

A complete and beautiful three-dimensional symbol manifested in front of me, with sounds and geometric proportions. I knew this was the key from some time in my distant past.

I was on the other side of the lake. There I was shown more details about the Earth elements, and also rhythmic breathing and other ways to bring that depth of information back.

These out-of-body trips lasted only a few weeks but the technical information I learned become invaluable to me later on in my journey.

Chapter 13

SPEAK NO MORE

I remained without speaking for almost six months.

I would transition from deep conscious sleep, to dream, to waking...all while experiencing the same "zero point" gaps that I had when traveling between dimensions.

I would shower, do yoga asanas and take a walk all before 5:00AM.

Then I would sit in full lotus, with a picture of my Guru in front of me, virtually motionless for at least two and a half hours. Then, I would do more yoga asanas, take another walk and eat some simple food. I worked from my room doing bookkeeping via mail for my clients (*via the mail* so I wouldn't have to speak very much to them.)

Then I'd repeat the same routine beginning at 4:00PM – asanas, a walk and in bed by 8:00PM to meditate, pray and surrender again until 9:00PM when I went through the gap into a light sleep, then conscious deep sleep (consciously in and out of dreams), then deep sleep again, then more dreams and then to waking state to repeat the routine again.

Our minds are great gifts to us as long as it is understood what the mind is for. Our minds function in specific ways. Ideally we use our minds as servants to our Hearts.

Ultimately, they become positioned appropriately, giving us information from the past as needed.

Prior to that appropriate positioning, we provide our minds with easy things to place our attention upon.

Intellectual or mental "breakthroughs" are only temporary

perturbations in our habit-based routines.

*Transformational events change your reality at the core,
a billion times more fundamental than any thought,
word or emotion.*

I presented to my mind during those silent days a photo of my Guru. I understood that photos have actual photons (which is where the word "photo" came from) which reflected off the person or objects in the photo; so in this sense my eyes were receiving little bits of the Guru from the photo. But more importantly, whenever I opened my eyes after deep meditation and prayer, I wanted my mind to first register with something which represented Love and a Paradise without suffering for all beings. The photo of my Guru represented that.

During the months of my twice-daily routine of prayer, meditation, gazing at my Guru and then simple activities, I noticed more and more the vicissitudes of my free will becoming more active.

My individuated self was still seeking. It was seeking even more understanding, more direction to serve and more insight into reality.

As the weeks rolled on, I noticed my desire to be completely One with my Guru. And yet, my mind continually reminded me that Unity already was, always will be, and always is here now.

Yet...the difference between the Event of Oneness I had in Santa Barbara, and my individual seeking self, was my current dilemma.

I was praying for a resolution of these differences. The Always Pervading Light and the changes of all things we are also living from moment to moment.

Everything is changing, always. And permeating within constant change is the true eternal non-changing Unity.

My mind translated the seeking into mental and verbal prayers:

"I want no separation with you my Guru!"

"Please let me melt completely into you!"

"I am here to serve AS you, for you and from you..."

"I have no desires of my own, except that they come from you..."

"You are The All and All."

"You are The Christ, The Buddha, all Liberation, all Manifestation, all Love, all Light, all Good, all the Time."

"You are Pure and Unconditional Compassion for all beings."

"You are not just the person in this photo...You are That which Fulfills the Purpose of all suffering, longing, seeking and surrendering."

"You are The Breathing Life Current of all life." "You are the Master Blueprint of all of Creation."

"Guiding Creation to its next Highest Level of Good is your NOW Reality."

"I am Thy servant. See me, Hear me, Feel me as Thy Servant. Show me how my Heart can beat As You..."

As I sunk my eyes into my Guru's picture, my practice of prayers actually became easier and easier because in a sense, I knew they were flawed.

How can I become something "new" in my current state of consciousness, which is not already in my current state of consciousness? I knew this.

So, I accepted my passion, my emotions, and the force of my motivated self, along with my utter surrendering of all passion, emotion and desire. I continued to unconditionally accept and love all of it.

All of this was experienced and projecting outwards toward my Guru's photo from the center of my chest. This was not a conscious decision, but I noticed it was there. None of the conditions of seeking, praying or relating came from my head area as I had often noticed in my past.

I was in my Heart.

> When the mind goes through the process of identifying itself as thoughts; when emotions are able to be loved and allowed completely; when every sense of one's life is accepted and released, then the Grand Paradox begins to resolve.
>
> The Paradox of the supreme and unchanging Bliss begins to show itself in everything.
>
> There is no resistance to the most mundane moment of the day – any moment of complete boredom or discomfort, or to the most profound, ecstatic, mind-opening and Heart-bliss moment of realization.
>
> Neither becomes more nor less than the other.

So the days continued with my routine. My basic bodily needs were being met (air, water, food, shelter, toilet and shower); my mind had an object for its priority (My Guru); and my emotions vacillated without resistance or concern. I remained within my heart noticing the dilemma of the feeling of separation between liberation and bondage.

One morning during the time after my meditation and prayers, I opened my eyes as usual, gazing as I had done countless times at my Guru's picture.

"Where are You now, my Guru?"

"You left your mortal coil in 1948, all that I have are your photos, your writings and the feeling of you. But where are You now? You showed up to guide me back from The Light [in 1979]. How wonderful. Thank You. But, I want You now! Are you real now, or shall I again release this illusion and accept all that is, just as it is? Are You *only* a projection for my mind? From my mind? I know even the photos of You will at some point decay and disappear along with my body, this very Earth, the sun and even the entire universe. I know this. I am fine with this, but if You are more than that, show me where You are at now. What dimension? Do You reside with the symbols? With the other Holy Beings, Archangels and Ascended Masters...or beyond?

Where are You, who are You, what are You!?"

No response. It was done. I released all of these questions. I am in this body; my heart is beating; I let go completely. I let go of all need to know, or need to resolve these questions.

My breath would usually stop after such pleadings. My mind would generally stop any of its thoughts. The boundaries of my body and psyche would become unperceivable. And then, it would all start up again and I would transit to activities with a drink of water into the day, to my computer to the book-keeping for my clients, to do the laundry, or whatever else.

This time none of that happened.

My breath had stopped, yes, but this time for some reason I couldn't inhale!

I couldn't take an IN breath! My heart began to race. I began to panic. This was not right. This wasn't the way I expected to die this time; I was choking for breath and all the reflexes in my body were thrashing for oxygen. I literally could not take a breath; my lungs remained empty.

My eyes were open and bulging. My chest felt like it was caving in. It was horribly painful and my body was panicking. Was I having a heart attack?

I began to collapse, my head curling over toward my legs. Would this be it? Would I die again, right here and now? Because of the intense effort my lungs made trying to breathe, this was not going to be an easy death. I began to black out.

Suddenly I felt something familiar. Bright, Loving, and Ecstatic.

I struggled to look up.

My Guru, fully embodied, sat right in front of me.

"See now where I reside?"

As soon as I heard the words I took my desperate IN breath. And as I breathed IN, HE collapsed, literally BACK into my own Heart, filling my lungs with both oxygen and the complete Union and resolution of all conflict.

"I am This. You are That. All This is That" became a reality and remained as my effortless being for several months without cessation.

It wasn't a concept or belief. It was a complete reality.

The first thing I lived after my breathing began again was simply looking around my room. Everything I looked at for more than a couple of seconds I completely *became*.

I looked at my turntable and I felt and knew everything about all the elements and components. I looked at the crystal stylus and saw every detail of the crystal – how the crystal vibrated, and how it transduced the vibrations into electrical impulses, into the amplifier and into vibrating acoustic signals which in turn vibrated my ears, and so on as music. I understood it all.

I put my attention on the floor, the walls and the sky outside. I became each of them.

I walked outside and down the street. Everything was alive "as me."

Then...I saw the first human, an elderly African-American lady walking home from her shopping, pushing her little personal shopping cart. One of the wheels on the cart was broken, which made a clicking sound upon every turn of the wheel.

I instantly became her...feeling her troubled past, her fear and her pain. My compassion and love for her was infinite. My love for her was the same Love which emanated from The Light, from The Guru and from Complete and Eternal Oneness. My love for this woman was no different.

"Good day Madam," I said.

I was her, yet I was in a different body reflecting her Truth, her Love, her completeness to herself. My mind now only functioned as a record-keeping mechanism and had become a servant to all of this; it could no longer project any separate realities. It was only able to bring past memories, impressions and information as necessary.

I desired nothing. There was nothing more to do except to love everything completely via the process of the mechanics of creation. This process always manifests as the three things – the subject, the object, and the process of awareness which bridges the two. Yet, the three are, in Truth, One, Eternal – never less than, more than or separate from – always limitless within the boundaries of the Cosmic Play. Three from One. One always as the Three.

My "body/mind/emotion/spirit" point of view was alive as the "play" itself.

The lady looked at me, startled. She was terrified. She immediately filled up with fear.

I just stood there loving her. I didn't dare to come closer though. I knew she was thinking, "Who is this guy?"

"What does he want from me?"

"Maybe he's going to rob me! I can't trust him at all!"

I spoke softly, "It's a nice day, isn't it?"

That was it. She took off with her personal shopping cart as fast as she could. The click-clack of the broken wheel is all I heard as she sped over the hill and off to "safety."

I understood. There was no concern. Without thinking I held my hand up and felt an energy connect with her – a healing energy, a blessing of sorts. I was not really "doing" this; my hand raised up and it happened.

I simply kept walking looking at the grass, looking at the street lights and at the cars on the road. All a wonderful play of diversity.

I remained in this state constantly and without interruption for nearly four months. It was during these times that I regularly left my body and visited the various higher domains, again without any hoopla or special interest. The celestial domains were just different neighborhoods. All was God.

I wrote and journaled. The symbols of the English language became a carrier wave for the various points of view of each day. I wrote about my bookkeeping clients, their auras, their patterns, their wants and desires. I wrote about the constant broadcast of Love from the Masters in the higher dimensions. I wrote about the sacred geometries and faster-than-light field generators that had been activated for this time of Earth.

Is the falling of the redwood seed truly random? Is the seed, now firmly surrounded by the dirt and decaying leaves of the soil, really on its own?

When the seed breaks and the sprout springs forth, does its nervous system really know which way is toward the sun?

When the sprout begins to grow, and receives the sun's photons, the carbon dioxide from the air, and then transforms those minerals from the soil with each photon and each carbon dioxide molecule into a green stem...what is really happening?

At each stage there are Laws which become active. They are like chords on a piano, latent but ready to become music.

The keys on a piano become music when a higher intelligence participates with them. For the piano, it is most often a human being, and for the benefit of those in the local proximity, hopefully a human being who knows about Chopin or Bach, or Keith Jarrett.

Music is not mechanical. It is never the same, and it is geared toward "new-ness" – something created that was not there before.

For a seed, the higher intelligence is Nature itself. And Nature has precipitated itself into certain "field frequency patterns." Nature spirits, plant devas, the elementals and such, are those beings who know the patterns of fields – for specific manifestations of creation.

As above so below. Fractal geometry remains the same no matter how deep into the structure you zoom.

The earth was a seed.

The seed had all the frequencies to become a paradise.

Not every seed becomes a tree, even though every seed has the potential to become a tree.

The original earth was a seed that developed quite a bit, but then got disrupted. The Heart center of the earth itself (and therefore all the human beings on the earth) became dormant. All were unable to continue to grow – at least in accordance with their potential. The earth then, by Law, and all the humans on it, simply recycled itself.

It re-seeded itself.

All gardeners want their gardens to express themselves to their highest potential! It is part of the happiness of the gardener to see the realization of the many beautiful flowers, and the many fruits ready to give of themselves in the great cosmic scheme of things. These desires are not from lack. No, they are as innate, intrinsic and alive as the fundamental fabric of creation itself.

From the current time/space reference point of all of us reading this, it has taken this second chance for Earth a long, long time to happen – millions of years. From the reference point of the Master Gardeners of this planet, it's only been a few months – a new season.

Humans have successfully gone through all the required stages to live and enjoy their creative potentials in harmony with all others on this planet, without cruelty, abuse and purposeless suffering!

It is a precious time! A golden opportunity for the Power of Love.

The awakening of Earth itself to a condition of Love instead of fear is part of the grand design of things.

We humans are quite naturally afraid. We have found that, at least temporarily, we can secure our safety and comfort with walls – both real and mental.

"Keep me ME. I don't want to transform into a 'new' human!"

This is actually the way we are all supposed to feel. Yet each of us knows there is something more. We believe, at least in the secret crevices of ourselves, that true liberation from suffering and cruelty is not only possible on this planet, but is its true design.

One of the most profound journeys revealed information about the mechanics of the change from one systematic state of matter to another. I was shown the discrete portals and connecting linkages between vibrational structures, like hallways between different rooms of manifest realities. The dominant factor governing the exchange of information from one "room" to another...was time.

I saw and wrote about the mechanics of miracles – for instance, the miracles of each human birth beginning with the fertilization of an egg. Science has done an amazing job in identifying all the miraculous changes the human body goes through from conception to birth and then, although at a slower pace, the still rapid changes from an infant to a toddler and so on. What the science books currently limit to chemistry will someday include the fields of information containing previously structured yet continually evolving blueprints. These blueprints are not like the blueprints for a house or car because in addition to the predetermined structures, there is always an ever-changing and evolving set of opportunities, and at some points in our lives, responsibilities to co-create not only our own bodies, but our entire life reality.

During the "descension" from pure Light in 1979 – "The Event" – at one point "I" experienced a domain full of beautiful mandalas, sacred geometries, and symbols. In 1981 more information about the 108 quantum codes was revealed to me. The codes are like discreet portals, or better put, geometric configurations at play in both the evolution of physical life and the evolution of consciousness itself. Each portal allows or disallows information to be exchanged or downloaded from a higher state potential to a lower state according to the governance of time, according to their season. The portals do not create the information, they allow it. In some cases a portal had been closed, or almost closed, for millions of years. I didn't know there were 108 of these "conduits" until years later, after I had the thought that I should simply count them. I had heard about the cosmic number 108 many times before, but the fact that the codes added up to this number blew my mind. I have since come to find that there are 108 sacred natural energies that we now draw upon using our Quantum Code Technology. Found everywhere in nature, these codes compose the fabric of the living world, including our biofield as living organisms. These codes serve as the baseline of optimal living. When modern day stress interferes with the interconnectedness between our biofield and our expressed lives, we lose efficiency, vitality, and overall quality of life. QCT clarifies, re-establishes, and enhances that innate connection, revitalizing our healing ability, creativity and our maximum life potential.

In another journey, I was shown the miracle of water and its secrets for life on planet earth. The 108 gateways continually allow information to transfer from higher states of consciousness and healing...into our water! I remembered how water played such a special role in the Christian Church. The second verse of the Christian Old Testament reads, *"Now the earth was formless and empty, darkness was over the surface of the deep, and the Spirit of God was hovering over the waters."*

In addition to the information I received regarding the potential of water, I was shown that the only way my body had healed and continued to live after my death in 1979 was via the information allowed into the water inside my body.

I also wrote about things of which I had no idea the meaning, according to the mind which followed me around.

But the True point-of-view was always so much greater than my mind. My mind would go to "sleep" during what is called deep sleep. Yet, my "subjective observer" never slept, nor had to. The Pure subject, of which "Robert" had become associated with, had no needs, no desires and no motives, and no agendas or resistances.

And yet, the gardener has a purpose. Let humans enjoy their differences AND Unity. We are one grand body with many parts.

I wrote about my two hands. Would one of them compete with the other to deliver food to the "one mouth?" How absurd. Why are we fighting each other over things? Why would one hand cut off the other for food? It knows that if the other hand bleeds to death, it will be the death of itself. It would just be a matter of time.

I also wrote about my Heart understanding and compassion for humanity. How wounded we all are. How many times we've seen and been subjected to intense suffering and terror. How many times we've shaken our fists upward to God in anger. I understood how many of us (me included) would call out, "How could you allow this, God?"

"There is cruelty and abuse happening somewhere right now! Why?"

Remarkably, I wasn't worried about this. I knew the Truth, and I knew each of us also knew it. Eventually the suffering would disappear. All badness to the family of humanity would resolve.

> *One of the most remarkable ways the Universe can balance itself, is using Time. Within the greater Whole of All, time is not fixed. It can change past events.*

I lived moment-to-moment with no real desire. I responded to hunger, and ate. I responded to thirst, and drank. I responded to the body's need for rest, and slept. I responded to the need to pay my rent, and worked to earn enough money. I had no sexual desire, but was always living more than any past pleasures – on any level.

I had no motivation for anything personal.

The "I" was like one molecule of H_2O in the vast ocean.

My father, Robert Wesley Williams in 1945, after his five years of combat against the Japanese during World War II. He left the army with a Purple Heart, a Patuan with 3 Bronze stars, the Asiatic Pacific Metal, the Philippine Liberation Medal and the Presidential Combat Infantry Badge of Honor. My dad never stopped looking out for the enemy.

This was the view from the hole I dug in my back yard in 1963. I was sitting at the bottom and took this shot of a friend. It was my refuge and a place for Jing and me.

From left to right, here are my sister Cheryl, my mother Mary, and my indian grandmother Vera Sebolt in 1968.

Here I am playing my saxophone in *The Arroyo High School Stage Band* in 1971.

This is me conducting my high school choir in 1971.

Here is my mother in her Cherokee tribal dress, in 1970.

This was a gig with *Hot Ice* in 1972 at the famous attorney, Melvin Belli's home.

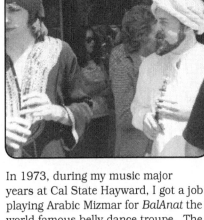

In 1973, during my music major years at Cal State Hayward, I got a job playing Arabic Mizmar for *BalAnat* the world famous belly dance troupe. The only condition (in addition to memorizing about a half dozen songs on the Mizmar) was that I had to wear a turban, although they frowned that my long hair always hung down.

I was a total "hippy" with long hair in 1973, but as a member of the *Musician's Union Local 510*, I was able to march with the union band for $15 per event.

This is *BalAnat*, the world famous belly dance troupe, in 1973.

Here is our band *Hot Ice* in 1974.

Here is Danny Pateris, my sax teacher ("Open the Gates") in 1974.

Here I am in 1975 at Cal State Hayward.

Here are my sister's husband Max, my sister Cheryl, my mom, and I the day I was initiated into Transcendental Meditation in 1976. "I found my Guru!" I had written in my diary.

This was taken before I headed off to *Maharishi International University* in 1977, with (left to right) my girlfriend Lisa, me, my mom, my sister and my sister's husband.

This was my room at *Maharishi International University* in 1977. I shot this so my parents saw that I was learning "real science" and not just meditation (all true). Note the title of the book *Elementary Physics*.

This photo is from my first year at *Maharishi International University*, with members of *The Welcome Band* in 1977. Left to right are John Wubbenhorst, me, Kathy and John.

Here is a shot from a gig I played with Paul Horn at MIU in 1977.

This was *The Bob Williams Quartet* performing outside at MIU in 1977.

Here is the back cover from *The Beach Boys* album I played on in 1977, called "The MIU Album."

In 1978, this was Mike Love's beach house in Santa Barbara. There were 14 houses on his land called "The Love Estate", where we all lived and worked for *LoveSongs Productions*, owned by Mike Love, Charles Lloyd and Ron Altbach.

Here's the famous Mike Love who gave me my break with *The Beach Boys*, and who I later worked for at *LoveSongs Productions* in Santa Barbara in 1978.

This photo I shot at an outdoor concert with *The Beach Boys* in Santa Barbara in 1978. I played baritone sax.

Here are Charles Lloyd and Jeri Rae at *LoveSongs Productions* in 1979. Charles and I were complete "bros" because we were the only ones in "Beach Boy Land" who liked (and played) jazz. Jeri Rae was a model for *Coppertone* and was a regular on *The Tonight Show with Johnny Carson*. She was one of the first ones concerned about my declining health.

This was a special day in 1978, when I performed on the television show *Dick Clark's American Bandstand* with *The Beach Boys*.

This was my view from the desk where I worked for Mike Love 1978, with the gold records in the background.

Here are Lisa and I on the right, with Tim, our full time mechanic at *LoveSongs Productions*, in front of Mike Love's Bentley.

This photo was taken at *LoveSongs Productions* in 1978, just a few months before my NDE (Near Death Experience). I am in the center.

Here I am in the garden at *LoveSongs Productions* in 1979, just a few months before my NDE.

After my NDE, here I am as co-owner of *The Spruton Sprouting Company* in 1981.

After my NDE in 1979, I started seeing psychic nutritional healer, Eileen Poole, in LA. This is me at one of my sessions, with a painting of Eileen in the background. She said at the time, that the only thing my body could digest was Bieler's Broth.

This is me at *The Spruton Sprouting Company* farm in 1981.

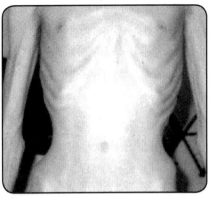

Here I am in my most emaciated state, right before I heard the Beings commanding me to dance.

This was me in 1984, after I had started dancing, gaining weight and coming back to life. This was my meditation spot next to my spiritual books and records to dance to.

Patti and me in 1993 at Kealakekua Bay in Hawaii. This was the vacation where we encountered the dolphin pod.

Chapter 14

DIMENSIONS

During this period of time, I would slip in and out of discrete domains of existence at will. I became intimately familiar with the different dimensions while remaining unified with all of them and the Eternal Now.

They were all as if a playground for entertainment. Like neighborhoods, they each have their distinctions, but in Truth each of us are functioning from all levels at once. It is only with the genesis of photons that time begins, and lower vibrational electromagnetic forces appear as Physics.

I journaled them:

First Dimension (1D) = total density/space

Second Dimension (2D) = total density and space

Third Dimension (3D) = physicality as defined by the conventional beliefs of physics. This includes the theory that nothing can travel faster (or at least not a lot faster) than light. We all remember this from Einstein's great equation, $E=MC^2$ with "C" representing the constant of speed of photons

Fourth Dimension (4D) = thoughts and thought forms, emotions, images, and subtle energy – a bit faster than light. We have very distinct fourth-dimensional bodies. We use these bodies to travel during sleep, dreaming, and so-called "super states" of consciousness. There are three levels within the fourth dimension – lower, mid, and higher – depending upon the amount of unconditional love that is being practiced by the resident beings

Fifth Dimension (5D) = less dense spiritual bodies integrated into soul groups more than individual souls. At this level the Law is Unconditional Love for All. There is no suffering in this domain. It is from this dimension where the blueprint for Paradise resides and which is now more than in the past, beaming the codes for humanity's next higher level of evolution. There are many benevolent beings who reside here, including some of our closest guides and angels

Sixth Dimension (6D) = sacred mathematics, geometric forms and bodies of sacred wisdom

Seventh Dimension (7D) = Creator Gods and Goddesses

Eighth through Twelfth Dimensions = orbs of vast unimaginable and incomprehensible Love, Purpose and Grace within the millions of Universes created

One aspect of the fourth dimension which is extremely relevant to this time of Earth, is what are called "thought forms" or "thought clusters."

A "thought form" is the energy created and sustained each time a sentient being thinks a thought. Often when a psychic is reading a person, they are reading the thought forms accompanying that person both in 4D and in 3D. Conversely, any sentient being can pick up on thought forms and, if not paying close attention, think that the thought has really originated from itself.

Have you ever noticed how some thoughts just spring in our minds and we think, "Wow, I just had an interesting thought." And then a few days later, or maybe a month or two, other people start talking about the same idea or thought. This is also why inventors and explorers freak out when they discover something new. History has shown that unless they hurry up and get it published, built, or make some kind of "my" claim on it, others will soon "get there first."

Another thing about thought forms is that modern psychologists have determined that our conscious minds can recall, record or recognize a maximum of forty thoughts (bits of information) per second. That's a lot unless you consider that they've also determined that our unconscious minds record and recognize over eleven million thoughts (bits) per second. What a difference!

If we consciously begin to project, control and/or recall certain thoughts, I have found that we are able to influence the thought forms which follow us around, and therefore influence our lives.

The idea of changing or being freed from our preconditioned thought forms is the basis of the great books on mind over matter, such as *Think and Grow Rich* by Napoleon Hill, and such movies as *The Secret.*

However, what I discovered is that there is a major limitation with the strategic influences on thoughts. Thoughts and thought forms are subject to mass influences from thought clusters.

Thought forms are a bunch of accumulated and unresolved energy packets created primarily by human minds and collective beliefs. For example, there was a time not that long ago that the earth was considered flat. Currently, most human beings on this planet think the earth is spherical, like a ball. When most humans think "Earth" today, (no matter what the language) they think of a globe; they no longer think of something flat that you can walk off of if you get to the end.

When a young child hears the word "earth" he or she not only begins to associate ideas picked up from the person speaking the word, "earth" but they also tap into 4th-dimensional thought forms about Earth via a Law called "sympathetic resonance." Thought forms are not formed from language (or verbal reality); they are more fundamental than that. Thought activates or pulls "files" from our minds, containing words from whatever language we think in.

Think of a huge flock of birds all flying together. Why are they all flying together? Because each individual bird instinctually knows that the flapping thing right next to it is very, very similar to itself. "Birds of a feather flock together."

Thoughts form "clusters" and stay together like the birds. They have basically the same vibrational components or resonance, no matter what language each individual mind uses to track it.

When we really come up with a so-called original thought, then there is either very little resonance in the existing thought clusters, or none at all. A lone bird! We have a hard time holding on to that thought. The reason is that the new thought has very little to resonate with until other thoughts of the same or similar vibration form around it.

Have you ever had a new thought and couldn't wait to write it down, lest it be lost?

Working as a musician with Brian Wilson of *The Beach Boys*, we all *knew* when he tapped into something really new. The new song or sound did not trigger any of our past memories of the hundreds of thousands of songs we had previously heard – nothing prior to reference from, even though we had been listening to music all our lives. Whether this something "new" from Brian felt good or not is another part of this investigation. It's not just the "newness" that makes us feel excited, it's whether it resonates with something from a "higher" dimension. Any time we connect more clearly with a higher dimension that is in line with The Innate Intelligence or the more whole and loving domains of reality, we receive energy from that dimension. This energy is pure life-force. This is what causes us to get "the chills" or goosebumps. Those are actually caused by "free electrons" and "free photons." The energy into our bodies from such connections do not come from food, water or air. They come from our higher vibrational bodies that conduct energy directly, without the need for food, etc.

Look at the following illustration:

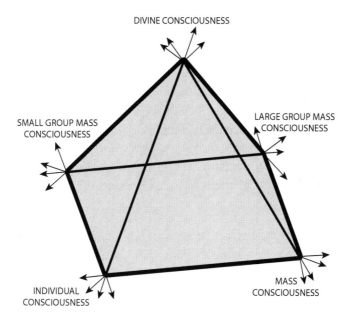

Individual consciousness, you or I right now, is depicted on the lower left. When we think a thought, it will resonate with mass consciousness depicted on the right. Mass consciousness is the sum total of all human beings who have many times thought that same or similar thought and therefore, have given it consistent sustaining power in the 4th dimension. Large group consciousness, upper right, also influences your thoughts, but a bit more of the particular associations in your individual life, such as "I am an American." The next are the small group consciousness influences such as "I am a Californian" or even smaller groups you are in, such as I am a stamp collector.

So when you think, "Earth" each thought cluster you unconsciously or consciously associate with will not only color, influence and define for you what the thought "Earth" is to you, but everything associated with your concept of Earth.

You can see that if there was nothing higher than our own thoughts that evolution would quickly stop. Why? Because right now, and at least for the last ten thousand years, the primary cluster of thoughts defining who we are as individuals has been in *contrast* to other individuals and their 3D and 4D differences.

"I am this, he is that. He and I are different. Does he want something from me? Is he going to take my food and leave me hungry? I must be careful, because there's not enough to go around and he may take what I know is mine. If I allow him to overtake me in some way, I may not get the mate that I am attracted to, or worse, others may cast me out of the community and I will be all alone in the wilderness. I may die and my genetic imprint will die with me. I must survive at all costs. How I act around this guy – especially when others are watching – is a serious affair. I must do whatever I can think of to protect myself in case he is an enemy. And, until he proves himself a friend, he is an enemy..."

These thought forms were absolutely necessary for our ancestors who were competing for food in the wilderness – and even for people today who need to compete for food and shelter because others are taking advantage of them, or are even killing them.

How can we get out of this state of affairs on planet Earth?

The answer is, as individuals we can't...unless we find an isolated community and live away from the masses. There are actual communities that I've visited physically, that have done this and they are doing great. But how can we initiate a globally reaching upgrade?

Let's look at the top of the pyramid diagram. "Innate Consciousness" or "Divine" Consciousness is there. It doesn't matter whether you call this state Christ or Buddha or God or Universal Law. All those thoughts and words are allowed there. None of them are rejected. However, at certain times the influences from this super level override ALL sentient beings' thoughts and beliefs. This level, depending upon which "wave" or cycle of influence is active, overrides all individual and mass influences on the planet combined. This is the phenomenon of mass transformation – either a mass of cells, such as in the caterpillar transforming each cell into a butterfly, or a race of beings transforming themselves into their next highest level of potential.

For now, the Divine level is still giving a whole lot of freedom of thought to the subsequent levels and down to you and I as individuals. However, a huge wave from this level has been building up slowly but surely and can be seen by some to be fast approaching the shore of humanity.

For example, for you right now reading this book, I know that you cannot think of hurting someone, or if the thought comes into your mind it cannot stay long enough for you to act on it. Impossible. You've cultivated more sympathetic resonance with your higher potential and reality (from the fourth dimension and higher). At certain points of evolution, some things become impossible and other things become miraculously possible, and sometimes inevitable. The codes from the higher vibrational blueprints create such an influence that lower vibrational thoughts no longer have anything to resonate with. They die out.

Anything that is activated at the Divine Consciousness level will influence or absolutely change either disruptively or supportively the thought forms of the masses, large and small groups, and even individuals.

When this happens, a complete and often revolutionary thing happens on Earth. (This is similar to the "Hundredth Monkey" idea.)

When it was time for humans to understand and believe that the earth was not flat, but a sphere, then all of the thought clusters of "Earth is flat, Earth is flat, Earth is flat" were overridden by the new understanding. At first poor Copernicus was the only one (supposedly) who picked up on this and announced it to the masses. As you've heard, he wasn't received very well. This is necessarily the case. Thought forms are strong and form the foundation of individual identities. If we accept an entirely new concept of the earth, we must accept an entirely different concept of our individual identities.

The Divine influences are actual large waves of energy. Large in the sense that their peaks and troughs – which govern major shifts in mass consciousness – cover vast lengths of time. The individual and small group waves are a lot shorter.

Think of real waves in the ocean. Deep wave currents that start in the Indian Ocean take at least twenty years to hit the Atlantic. There are all kinds of smaller waves along the way that either ride on top of the large ones or are overtaken. We are like individual swimmers making our own little waves but when the big ones come, we can only succumb to them. At first, before the bulk of the wave hits us, we *can* – and most often do – *resist* the larger influences. At first we think we are countering the wave – at first we think we are stronger than it. In time however, the wave overtakes any efforts against the direction of the wave. We either perish trying to swim against it, turn the heck around or go with it.

When I was doing my various out-of-body travels, it took a lot longer in locations where there were a lot of people. The local thought forms of those folks created kind of a sludge of interference between the third and the upper parts of the fourth and fifth dimensions too. Once I got past those thought clusters though, it was easy.

Think of the pyramid diagram again. If you bypass mass consciousness and begin to resonate directly with the Divine/Innate levels, then those waves give you the "highest possible truth" for that moment because it is connected (linked) all the way down to this moment on our 4D and 3D levels.

Jesus said, "If two or more are gathered in my name, then I will be among you."

Why two or more? It turns out, that if two or more put their attention on anything that is resonating at the Divine level, then Divine Beings that are recognizable to humans become available. Remember the rainbow is always there passively waiting until the proper relationships on the earth are established.

After a while, for those of us who become habituated with the fundamental reference point coming from the Supreme vibrational levels, we can walk into a chaotic crowd of people and not "lose ourselves." Another way to put it is that we don't lose our Power of Love. The more of us who awaken to this empirical truth, the easier it becomes for each of us.

Dear reader: *we have enough now!* There is only one more step to manifest the Power of Love.

Chapter 15

GABRIEL IS BLOWING HIS HORN

In my dimensional travels, I was shown that *"Gabriel is blowing his horn."* The waves set into motion a long time ago are reaching our shores. Just like a keen surfer who can feel the great waves coming, many of us are feeling it now, and have been feeling it for some time actually – many of us for the last 40 or 50 years.

So, just like the surfer who rushes to paddle out and takes advantage of the great waves to ride high with the awesome power of the ocean – of Nature – all we have to do is paddle out. Really, all we have to do is to put our attention on this wave. Before you finish this book, you will know exactly how to do that – if you don't already.

> *The waves are here. The possibility of a new consciousness for humanity is really at hand. If you want more evidence, simply look around at many organizations and people who are hopeful at the very least if not completely committed to this transformation. Or better, feel the silent depths of your Heart. It is there where we are hearing the call, the sacred silent sounds and the resonance of the awakening.*

In 1981 I had no concerns about waves or even forms. We, I, Robert, was simply breathing moments of unity. Everything was full of everything else. Everything made sense in both directions of time. Even though I saw all the suffering, fear, cruelty and abuse, "I" "We" remained untouched. There IS a reality where that is completely true. This is a more whole and true reality.

I could only love and bless each moment. And when I saw something that held my attention for more than a few seconds, my hand would raise and some mysterious energy would leap out of it toward the object. Again, a paradox. What was going to what? I cared not. It was what it was – a mysterious dance within the play of time, cycles, phases and creativity in motion.

When I would walk into a room or place, usually a grocery store or somewhere public since I didn't have a social life, electronics would often crash. People would sometimes get very agitated and even angry for no apparent reason. I soon learned to modulate my energy field. Again, the paradox of unity along with the thought of compassion for those parts of myself – the people and things in different physical bodies – that had yet to fully realize the freedom I was living. Those that were bound by the thought forms of mass consciousness.

One of the things about clairvoyance, seeing things other people don't see, is to think that either you're crazy or special. Most of the time when I was growing up and even up until the late 1980s I thought I was crazy. I knew I wasn't mentally retarded, or mentally ill in "severe" ways, but what is one to think when you say to someone, "Hey I just saw this or that," and they don't acknowledge what you've seen, and just look at you funny. After time, you just keep some things to yourself.

This is where it helps to read books and speak with people who share your experience. Clairvoyance has been around for centuries according to books written long ago. In the early 1980s I purchased as many books as I could on the following subjects, 1) symbols and sacred geometries, 2) religions and ancient cultures, and 3) clairvoyance.

Once I started to read books by C.W. Leadbetter and Alice Bailey, I felt a lot less crazy. At last I was reading not only about people seeing things in the "subtle domains" but descriptions of what they all meant. Some of the colors and formations I saw were self-evident; I learned by repeated experience. For instance, whenever my father's temper would explode, I would see a sharp dark red color emanating from his solar plexus. When he was loving to us, I would see different colors, but this certain hue of dark red always meant explosive anger.

> *Until we realize the fundamental truth of who we are,*
> *which is complete and ultimate Love permeating all*
> *things in all time, space, creations, dimensions, forms*
> *of consciousness, forms of life, people, places, and things,*
> *then "who we are" collapses into what is recognized*
> *objectively by our mentally-created beliefs and individuated*
> *consciousness. Reality is governed and determined*
> *by a supposed "subject," "I," experiencing a supposed*
> *separate "object," "it."*

I learned to control my subtle and celestial vision. I had to communicate with people in this time and space. If I saw too much of a person's aura, their own thought forms of pain and misery, their own prisons of conditioned patterns, I literally could not hear their physical words or remain present enough to talk with them.

I learned to "tune everything down." Again, not because I didn't like those conditions or didn't understand them, but only as an appropriate response to the people and environment around me. Appropriate because the feedback from the Divine level (the top of the pyramid) instantly supported and allowed it. I really had no choice. If I attempted something that, for whatever reason, was not resonating with the Divine levels, I just couldn't follow through with it, whether it be a thought, word or action.

In hindsight, since I had no personal desire, no motivation and felt no concern, it was obvious why I had to topple back down.

I was living in only the upper three Chakras, along with my fully alive and open Heart.

All good, except there are seven Chakras, not four.

It was time to descend, my unity abruptly ended.

It was my physical body.

I was dying once again. I had finally studied my body in the mirror and saw my skin and eyes were completely jaundiced. I was sunken and gray and I looked terrible.

For the first time in over a year, the pain overtook me. It was not just my bodily pain however, it was the pain of every human being on Earth. Although I had the point of view of unity, beyond all suffering, I had disconnected from the pain of the separate self, the separate body, the separate lives we all remember and identify with. This would have been fine if it was really my time to physically die. It wasn't. I couldn't swim against the waves of "the purpose for coming back" into my body in March 1979.

All at once as I looked at the reflection of my body in the mirror, my mother's sobbing at the abuse she endured flashed before me. I saw my father's terror at the face of unspeakable torture and horror during his time in the army in Southeast Asia during World War II. I remembered how my sister had sustained the constant verbal abuse of my father and how Lisa had described how she was raped and beaten before she had met me.

And these were just the people close to me. I collapsed and began to sob. The sobbing was relentless. I had not sobbed or even had an emotion for almost a year.

Now my journey switched from the domains of Unconditional Love, Freedom, dimensional travels and The Light, to darkness – into to the hate, brutality, abuse, rage and worse realities still part of humanity. I was no longer "above" it. Deep, deep down I went; my body began to convulse. I somehow got to the bathroom to vomit, have diarrhea and eventually fall onto the bathroom floor, trembling.

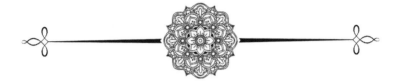

Chapter 16

DANCE!

I was completely alone now, except for John Wubbenhorst who would stop by once a week or so to make sure I was still alive. Mom continued to send me $500 per month without my father knowing. That was what I used for all expenses.

I never slept more than a few hours maximum. The physical discomfort was beyond anything I ever imagined possible. I couldn't eat anything without either vomiting it out, or having so much abdominal pain that all I could do was crouch by the toilet, moaning. After an hour or two it would subside enough for me to crawl back to my bed.

I kept repeating to myself, "Don't think, just act. Just keep doing one thing after another."

What will I do now? I will crawl to the sink, stand up, drink water and then get to the bed. All aspects of my body were in some range of pain from "7 to 10+." The feeling of my blood being poisoned, with everything aching, every cell screaming, every skipping heartbeat sending sharp pain to my head. My ears were constantly ringing; I was always dizzy and disoriented. I couldn't complete a sentence without stuttering or forgetting how the sentence started.

John kept asking if he should take me to the hospital or to a doctor.

Just like I said to the folks back in Santa Barbara, I always said, "No."

And then one day, John said he was moving to India for at least a year to study Bansuri with the Master Teacher Hariprasad Chaurasia.

"Good-bye my brother. You will become even greater than you are now!" I said.

"I love you brother. I trust our Guru will take care of you now."

"Jai Guru Dev!" I said.

I realized how much I would look forward to his visits. I didn't have to say anything. He would come over and practice his flute or try to get me to eat something. I loved him.

Now, weeks turned into months of complete aloneness. The pain seemed to deepen. I prayed every day for The Light to come back – for death – for release from the sins I concluded I must have committed in some past life to be in such torture. I must have once been Adolf Hitler, I thought.

No more Light. No more out of body experiences. No more angels, and no more communication from beings of the other dimensions. Just my decaying, suffering body, some food, the bathroom and the bed.

I had to make a decision every day. Do I urinate in bed or crawl to the toilet? It only took once wetting my bed to never decide that way again. But to get to the toilet was almost unbearable. I would scream in pain, then moan as I hyper-ventilated while I forced my body to move.

I must admit, when I finally got to the toilet to urinate, I felt a temporary release! Ahhhh! But as every human knows, it is a short-lived sensation.

I never defecated in bed. I'm glad. Having a bowel movement in the toilet was even a bigger, albeit temporary sense of relief. But that was only once every ten days or so.

One day the toilet stopped up. I made it down the two flights of stairs and to the yard outside. There was a snow storm going on and the bitter cold actually felt temporarily comfort-

110

ing; everything became numb. I so prayed while I was releasing myself on the frozen bushes to be taken right there. Numbness and a quick sense of release was my bliss for a few moments, so desperate and exhausted.

But my breath kept going. I had absolutely no clue as to why. There was no Light whatsoever anymore. Maybe it never really happened? Maybe someone had drugged me without me knowing? Why did Jing have to leave me without him so many years earlier? How would I ever heal? Even if that happened somehow, what would I start doing to earn money, to enter the world again?

Every thought was a horrible experience. My thoughts only contained memories of either past blissful times, or anything I ever did which I regretted. The memory of the girl I kicked on the playground in the third grade would start and repeat over and over and over, and only stop with a sharp pain somewhere in my physicality which would either override the broken record or replace it with something else. Sometimes these repetitive thoughts and images would go on for days. I would scream.

Over more than four long years the thoughts slowly mitigated. Or maybe my mind just decreased in its capacity to register them. The ringing in my ears also lessened. The pain was still there but certain things seem to hurt less.

It had been four years since The Light left and the brutal registry of body pain overcame everything.

It was one of those decision moments again. Should I pee in bed or walk to the bathroom? I knew the answer, which began the ordeal of moving my body out of bed.

Suddenly out of the blue, and in a voice I had never heard before, I heard the strong yet gentle word, "Dance."

It stunned me. I stopped and looked around.

Who said that??

"Dance," it repeated.

I then knew I was hearing it inside my head, but unlike any voice of my past.

I made it to the bathroom and back, but this time I listened for the voice...still completely startled by the two times I had heard it just minutes before.

I got back into bed. Several minutes passed.

"Dance!" This time it was louder and more emphatic, yet still gentle and...kind?

What on Earth? What does this mean? What in the world could the word "dance" mean?

"DANCE!"

For a moment I thought it was a cruel joke from some dark entity, but almost immediately I knew it couldn't be. There was Love behind it. "Oh my God!" I cried out. There was that feeling of Love every time I heard the voice. Perhaps if I had more energy or an emotional connection, I would have cried. But the tears would have to wait.

"DANCE...DANCE...DANCE!"

I stumbled into the living room. Almost like a programmed robot I thumbed through my albums until I found it.

Michael Jackson's *Thriller.*

I skipped to the sixth track, *Billy Jean.* I turned it up loud. I felt the famous base line thumping my feet and then my whole body – MY WHOLE BODY, PAIN AND ALL!

I began moving to the music, slowly and stupidly awkward at first, then the third miracle of my life happened.

112

A tremendous RUSH of life-force came DOWN from the top of my head through my body, through my feet and went into the earth.

I was naked and dancing with the beat and gesturing with Michael's lyrics, "You...but I'm not the one!!"

I began to sweat profusely; I kept dancing; the next track, *Human Nature* continued the miracle.

I knew all the words and began singing along with my pelvic-thrusting dance moves! The longer I danced, the freer I became.

The album ended. I collapsed on the couch, but not like the collapsing of the last four years. It was an ecstatic collapse. I turned on my side and started laughing until I had to stop because it hurt so bad. But then like a giggling adolescent, I laughed again. I didn't care about my stomach pain. I laughed more and then...went to the deepest sleep I had had in many, many years.

I woke up – and the pain was back – blazing, pounding and scorching pain.

But there was lightness in my Heart. I smiled at the pain while I went to the bathroom. Then took some water, rice and some red meat. I took a bath with Epsom salt.

I was about to get out, when my intuition kicked in – for the first time since the yellow eyes looked back at me from the mirror, six months after The Event, No Separation, No Difference, No Other, and four years four months prior to this particular bath.

Accept the pain.

Love the pain.

I understood. Accept and Love the pain without condition. Without any resistance to the pain, or anything else or attachment to any concept from any past memory or anything, whatsoever.

Accept everything – EVERYTHING – including all the suffering on the planet, in the astral worlds, and in all other places. Accept everything exactly in the present moment exactly how it is. If the mind brings up ANY THOUGHT, then accept that, along with the pain. Emotion? ANY EMOTION – accept that, no holding on, no letting go, and no moving away on any subtle or gross level.

Loving the physical pain became total loving. TOTAL LOVE.

I was no longer motivated to act, physically to "go somewhere," "stay somewhere," or "return to somewhere." There was no agenda at all. There was only Love.

This time, unlike the time in 1980, I WAS PAIN; I WAS BLISS; I WAS ALL EMOTION, AND ALL OF IT WAS LOVE. I WAS THE LOVER OF IT ALL, THE PROCESS OF LOVING IT ALL, AND ALL THAT WHICH I WAS LOVING. There was now a physical body, in pain, yes, but with, from, and as, THIS SAME LOVE.

As the days followed the nights, the clairvoyance began to return, and along with it all the suffering souls that I had abandoned in the astral kingdom. They fought me with a vengeance at first; they spewed out excruciating anger and howling.

I loved them. I loved and kept loving. I did not try to help them. I did not try to "do" anything. I loved.

Things changed, vexed and cycled without any plan, intention, reason or rhyme. I began gaining weight! The last time I had enough energy to step on a scale, I was down to 108 lbs. Very cosmic I thought, but heck, I was six-feet-three inches

114

tall! But after dancing, which for most people would have resulted in losing weight, I began to gain. I felt it.

John had returned from India and came over to see how I was doing.

"Bro-man, you're coming back!"

I had the odd habit of seldom putting on any clothes – since it was a rare event that I left the apartment, or that anyone visited me except John.

John was standing there looking at me naked.

"Bro-man, you still look like you're a walking skeleton, but dang, you look better!"

I ran to the scale and charged out telling John I was up to 123 lbs!

I asked him to bring his camera the next time he came over and to take a couple of photos of me. Perhaps it was intuition, perhaps hopeful thinking, but either way I knew I would never be that skinny again. When he came back, I was still naked.

"Put some damn clothes on, bro!"

"Too much hassle, bro...I'll just put a bag over my head," I suggested.

And then the "now infamous" photos which have horrified doctors and lovers alike were taken. A week later, John's wife came over to witness for herself my progress. Except this time, I put on clothes.

A month or two later I received a call from Kevin Slade and Mark Barlettani, two known healers and clairvoyants. "Your soul has been tapping us on our shoulders, Bob. It's time for you to join us in La Jolla, California."

I packed up and flew to San Diego within seventy-two hours. Ready for a new chapter of life, I bid Fairfield, Iowa farewell.

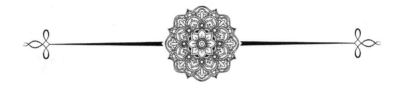

Chapter 17

DANCE REVISITED

Mark was a remarkably adept clairvoyant and he could read auras with incredible accuracy. About a month after *Coherence Industries* began, he charged into my office and said, "You need to have sex!"

"What?" We had not had anything close to this kind of conversation before.

"Sex, man! When is the last time you had it – with a woman, masturbation, anything!?"

After the March 20, 1979 event, I lived without any sexual need or desire. And after the 1981 event with my Guru, I lost all desires whatsoever. It was now 1986.

"You're still way too high in your upper Chakras, Robert! You gotta get DOWN and sex is one of the best ways to do it. I'm not talking about Tantra or lofty spiritual sex! I'm talking about fucking!!"

I was stunned. It had been almost seven years.

"Kevin and I are driving you to the strip joint in San Diego *tonight*. I want you to go to the front row, pick out a dancer and have a 'one-on-one' with her!"

"What the heck is a 'one-on-one,' Mark?"

"Don't ask. We're going tonight. Take a fucking shower."

I was terrified. What if one of my meditating friends saw me there? I began to laugh. Wouldn't it be hilarious if I DID see one of my "good" meditating friends there?

When we arrived, Mark and Kevin literally kicked me out of

the car and sped off. It was just me and *Le Girls*, the premier all-nude strip club in San Diego.

Mark had instructed me to keep checking my libido and not to come back until I "felt it."

So in the club I went, directly to the front row. No alcohol is allowed in all-nude clubs so I ordered a lemonade. The seminude waitress gave me a suspicious look.

What impressed me was how comfortable most of the dancers felt. Then I understood; here they were completely in charge of a bunch of horny men, but they were safe and without concern for abuse. The huge bouncers flanked both sides of the stage and escorted each dancer on and off.

Any customer who began to get rude or out of hand, "Come to me baby! Rub your pussy in my face..." were quickly and sternly removed from the club. Those of us that weren't kicked out were "good boys," willing to abide by the rules, to look at naked women dancing and cavorting with us.

After each dancer had stripped, the announcer loudly blasted out calls on the PA system for "one-on-ones" with the now completely nude dancer. Just $20 is all it would take for a completely private one-on-one with...Danielle!

I raised my hand and Danielle gave me a wink while one of the huge guys escorted me to the back of the club into a room with a mirror, a chair, a little raised platform with another chair and a big clock.

Danielle came in and sat down on the platform. I saw her quiver as she looked furtively at me. She was nervous. She was young, and not so confident as she was on the large stage.

"What is your name, handsome?"

"My name is Robert, and I want you to know that I'm not here to have sex with you or even just to look at you."

"Sex is not allowed, handsome," as she glanced to the mirror which I now understood to be one of those two-way see-through kind. "But you can look all you want, and even jerk-off. I'd like that!"

"No Danielle, you don't understand. I have no sexual desire and the friends I work with made me come here to see if I can gain my libido back."

"Well, don't you feel anything?" She began to caress her breasts and pinch her nipples.

"No Danielle, and you don't have to do that."

She actually looked sad, and close to tears. I wanted to hold her and tell her how beautiful she was – including her sexy body, but so much more. I stepped up to the platform and immediately one of the big guys barged in and shouted, "no touching the models!"

He scared us both. I sat down, closed my eyes, and imagined loving her, hugging her, and even caressing her but without any personal agenda.

I opened my eyes and now she was crying.

"Who are you?" I asked.

"I'm nobody, Danielle. I'm nobody."

Then my third eye opened. I saw the most beautiful angel right above her right shoulder. The angel was bathing Danielle with golden and violet rays.

"I'm so sorry, I'm not supposed to cry here," she whispered.

"But it's okay; the big guy is not stopping us. Keep crying, dear Danielle."

"Who are you?" she asked.

"Nobody."

I knew the time was up when the same big guy who had stopped me from touching Danielle barged back in with a polaroid camera.

"Only another $20 and you can have your picture with sexy Danielle, man!"

I paid the guy, and he told me that now I could sit on the chair and she would sit on my lap. I felt her body and her sweat, and smelled her hair.

Click, the picture was taken. Danielle was quickly escorted out with the big guy while I remained alone for a few more minutes while the Polaroid developed. The guy came in and gave me the photo.

"You want the sexiest ladies, you know where to come, ha ha."

I looked at the picture.

On it was written, "Thank you handsome, whoever you are. Love, Danielle."

Chapter 18

COLLIN

After three years living with the Slade family which included seven-year-old Collin and his younger brother Austin, age three, I moved out of their home and in with my girlfriend, Shelley.

After being totally celibate for nearly seven years, I was now enjoying sex. Shelley was a Farrah Fawcett look-alike and loved sex. I wanted to practice Tantric and spiritual sex with her, but she would have nothing to do with it. The goal was orgasm, period. For me, nothing came close to the experience I had with Anandamayama after I had started dancing. But sex was fun with Shelley, and I had grown to understand humans for getting so caught up in the whole "release-seeking, chemical-producing seek-and-reward desires." Like all things, sexual intimacy can become a powerful carrier-wave of Love and Light. Like *all* things.

I had studied the auras of those who enjoyed sex on a regular basis. A bright orange and red colored energy would build up between the knees and the solar plexus, concentrated mostly right in front of the base Chakra on men, and just at the back of the base on women.

The energy would be pressing against the physical – wanting "out." Release was its objective, simple release. I explored with the energy in my own subtle body make-up and found that out.

Mark, Kevin, and Mark's girlfriend, Sonya met daily at the office...experimenting with meditating, dancing and laughing. We also saw "clients." The three (or four of us if Sonya joined in) treated their diseases, neuroses and other ailments.

Dr. Kevin always took the lead since he had the official DO degree. Often, Mark and I were in the other room working clairvoyantly on the person while Kevin did his doctor thing. I was always amazed at Kevin's fast ability to "see" someone's pathology. He would write on the client's notes after simply looking at the person's aura, "Left kidney about ready to pass stones...treat second Chakra ASAP."

It was a good time for me and only the second time in my life I felt understood. Although Jing had yet to return to my life, at least Mark and Kevin didn't think I was crazy, and they had had similar encounters with celestial beings growing up.

The three of us would take long walks around La Jolla, and whenever a being from the astral world would rush out at us from somewhere, we would stop and send it to The Light. Most beings around the cove and the shops on Coast Boulevard were benign. They were either from the upper astral or even from the fifth dimension. We loved watching the fifth level devas at the bakery delighting in the freshly baked breads.

Something sacred about making bread I thought must be the case, and then investigated. Before the grains got messed up with chemicals and mass production, bread was used spiritually and medicinally. And the beings associated with the healing are still here on Earth, although their abilities are drastically compromised because of the grain degradation and the lack of consciousness about the whole affair.

According to Kevin, Collin caught the flu on a Wednesday, April 13th. We were not very concerned. Like all children, Collin caught colds and ran fevers only to recover within a few days – a week max.

None of us, with all our psychic abilities and aura-reading skills picked up on anything at all unusual about Collin's flu.

The phone woke both Shelley and me up at 5:00AM. I instantly knew something was wrong. It was Mark calling from the Hospital. Collin was dead.

Until the Age of Love is stabilized on Earth, the unpredictability of death will continue. And worse, horrible things will continue to happen too – rape, torture, abuse and cruelty.

This is why you were born during this time. You have the codes in your heart, no matter what you're doing or thinking, they are already broadcasting out Love.

All you need to do is persist with this knowledge. Love yourself and others without any conditions whenever you remember to. You will find others who are doing the same. The phrase "Love is the Power" will ring stronger than ever.

We never found out the official reason for Collin's death. Since Kevin was a licensed physician, he somehow persuaded the ER doctor to record the cause of death as aspiration pneumonia.

Collin's body was cremated three days later.

David Cochran, one of the clearest and most accurate clairvoyants on the planet, said it was a brain tumor. Upon looking back, symptoms of a brain tumor had indeed shown up.

Kevin and Becky never fully recovered. Their youngest son, Austin became almost my full-time responsibility. He had just turned four.

I've never seen such hysteria. Kevin would run at full speed directly into the wall out of complete, crazy anger and utter misery. They both would yell, scream, cry uncontrollably and wail deep into the night. There was no sleep. How Austin processed this I have no idea. In the midst of his parents losing their minds, we would play with toy trucks in the other room, toys once shared with his older brother.

Kevin started smoking nonstop. He never forgave himself. How could the great clairvoyant medical intuitive who had healed people from stage-four cancer and worse...miss the symptoms of his very own son?

Had he brought Collin into the hospital for an MRI, the tumor might have been spotted.

> We can only say that the immense pain, despair, isolation, and unexplainable health problems are your sacrifice, until the Truth of Love outshines suffering and death. We love you so much for this sacrifice. Someday those memories will be completely repositioned in the Cosmic scheme of things.
>
> You have always been free of pain.
>
> You will awaken to this soon.
>
> The dream state of pain will become like a drop compared to the ocean of Love.

The guilt and shame would follow Kevin wherever he tried to go. He left Becky and me alone with Austin. He went to, of all places, Hollywood and started having a crazy affair with a zealot a block or two away from Hollywood Boulevard.

Becky, on the other hand, got involved with intense therapy. And eventually she got her MFCC license (Master of Family and Child Counseling).

There is an Angel of Death. I had seen him before. According to my mental projections, he carries a strange staff. He lurks. He comes in and out of places of great Light and places of great suffering, famine, disease and war. He goes in and out of common places, in grocery stores and on the streets – while we sing in the shower – while we are being held by our fathers.

Collin was dead. It happened. I saw it. It was the physical death of a precious child. But twenty years later I saw Collin holding Kevin, who himself had died of cancer. It was on another dimensional plane, yes, but I saw them together, alive and happy again. This is what happens time and time again after the tragedy of losing a loved one. Someday this will all change. The path of Love is the right path to lead us there.

During this time of Earth the Angel of Death has a very important role. He takes life from one state to another unexpectedly. His agenda seems completely indiscriminate to you. You think he's the devil or worse.

He is only serving this time of Earth.

The time for him is limited in his current capacity. It is possible that within your lifetime, his role will change. More peaceful, graceful and honorable transitions will be his service.

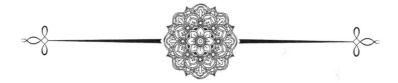

Chapter 19

THE CHEROKEE

My great, great-grandfather on my mother's side was a pure-blooded Cherokee Indian. It took my mother several years of painstaking research to prove this. Seabolt was his name and he actually walked and survived the infamous *Trail of Tears* trek from Florida to Oklahoma. Those that arrived at the place designated by the US government to become "The Cherokee Nation" had to pass certain requirements. First, the Cherokee Chief had to confirm that this man was indeed part of the Cherokee Tribe and pure-blooded. Second, the Indian had to answer a few questions to prove to the government that he was "civilized."

Senator Henry Dawes, who was one of the few pro-Indian congressman and key in the allotment of Indian land, was there and witnessed the signature of each confirmed Cherokee man. The original *Dawes Role* with only 100,366 signatures accepted (out of over 50 million Indians) is now on display at the National Archives and is individually status-supervised by the Bureau of Indian Affairs.

My mother was able, through birth certificates and other paperwork, to locate Seabolt's signature. Because of the nature of the treaty, any descendant of a man who signed the Dawes Role could become a member of one of the five "civilized" tribes. Each nation had an "almost" fully sovereign status within the US. Truthfully, it wasn't until Cher's hit *Half-Breed*, and the famous Marlon Brando called out for the rights of the American Indian at the Oscars, did the political status of the American Indian begin to change.

When I was seven years old, my sister, mother, and aunt drove from the Bay Area to the Cherokee Nation so my great-grandfather, also named Seabolt, could see my sister and I before he passed away. I was still too young to get what Indians were all about; my mother seldom spoke of her ancestry and spoke even less of the heart-wrenching persecution of the Cherokees. "Ethnic cleansing" was finally admitted formally by the US Government with apologies to each surviving tribe in 2000.

After a week of driving over 1800 miles in our 1956 Ford four-door, we arrived at cousin Sheila's house. My mother's sister's daughter lived in a little town called Spiro, Oklahoma – about an hour away from the Cherokee Nation lands. She could have lived on the land, of course since she was also a Cherokee, but as a new mother, she wouldn't have anything to do with it. Once we drove into Cherokee land I knew why.

The poverty, repression, alcoholism and disgusting conditions were overwhelming. Although only seven, I had never seen or imagined anything like it. At the same time, there was something about this place that reminded me of my encounters with Jing and the nature spirits in my own back yard.

Although the sad Indian plight is now well known to Americans, what is not...is the Indian knowledge of the land, elements, trees, plants and animal spirits. Much later in my life I returned to the Cherokee land and had an encounter with medicine man who - upon much reluctance shared some secrets with me. This was only after I had to prove to him with paperwork my relationship to the original Seabolt.

Back as a seven-year-old, I only remember the power I felt on Cherokee land, and the silent grief that prevailed among the residents. After a long wait, my mother brought Great-Grandpa Seabolt out to meet us. He was in an old and rickety wheel chair – a pathetic sight.

First my sister was introduced; he half smiled and shook her hand. I was next. Suddenly, I was transfixed by him. The energy in and around him seemed to grow with ferocity. He looked directly into me, his eyes completely alive, strong and warrior-like.

After he shook my hand, he placed his palm at the middle of my forehead and kept it there for what seemed like forever. Time stopped. With his hand still on my forehead, I saw one shimmering symbol in my mind's eye – a beautiful eight-pointed star symbol.

I would see the same symbol again, as the first of many I saw when I was descending back into my body after my Near Death Experience, 18 years later.

Great-Grandpa Seabolt finally removed his hand and everything went back to the previous sad and repressed state. His face again became lifeless; his eyes lost their luster as he peered back into nowhere.

> Deciding the fate of the planet is beyond the capacity of the human mind.

> Deciding the fate of specific races, cultures and information lies within human free will.

> As consciousness expands through the fourth (heart) energy center, appropriate collective decisions will become obvious if not self-evident. Actions will become more effortless as the Universal Laws of Heart Awakening become more and more active.

> Symbols remain only symbols, like music notation, until one understands. If one understands the symbol of the note "C," then a tone will emerge either from voice or instrument.

> When humanity reaches the critical tipping point of understanding, the symbology which has been appearing as far back as Paleolithic cave art, and in art in every culture and time period since then, will become understood. The

symbols are also present in the natural patterns of plants, trees, ocean waves and even human anatomical proportions.

And being a musician, I could immediately see that humanity will begin to understand the sacred symbols that begin to form the actual 108 energies that later became the basis to my work, the creation of the Quantum Code Technology.

Heart-based Love will blossom readily and quickly, as a reminder of who we really are as we attain our highest potential during our time on Earth.

My mother began working on establishing her official status as a Cherokee American Indian and was able to prove that her great-grandfather signed the official *Dawes Role*. It didn't matter how much your Indian blood was diluted by other races, as long as you could be traced back to the Dawes Role, you could become a member. My mother applied for my sister and I in 1978 and we were accepted.

I flew back to the Cherokee lands in 1992 and after many days of waiting, was introduced to one of the few remaining Cherokee medicine men. He eyed me carefully and looked over my paperwork even more closely. After he seemed satisfied, we began to walk away from his small plot of farm land and after several hours we arrived at a river. He washed his hands and face in it and motioned me to do the same.

When he began singing, I again saw the same symbol I had seen from Seabolt years earlier. This time it made more sense. It was a doorway into faster-than-light domains of the earth – again a way into the higher dimensions. It was exactly the same symbol I had seen in 1979. Then he motioned me to look behind myself, and I saw several Cherokees from past times (in their subtle bodies) observing us. In addition, I could also see the tree spirits very awake and with their very tall forms, blessing us.

When the medicine man and I arrived back at his farm, he sat down and motioned me to do the same.

"The Cherokees fought for the land more than for themselves. We saw what was coming. Don't worry about it. We are a dying culture. It is okay, but what we cannot let die is Mother – this Earth, The Mother, we cannot let die. Go back and do what you can do."

He then took both my shoulders in his powerful hands squeezing them together – empowering me. He spoke in Cherokee to bid me farewell.

As I thanked him and began walking back to my car – he then said something I totally didn't expect, "Do some sweat lodges!"

I knew he didn't mean with him or even with the Cherokees. The "white man" had commercialized sweat lodges back with Cher and the American Indian movement, a watered down version for sure.

A year later I was to spend two weeks with "Beautiful Painted Arrow" doing daily sweat lodges and being initiated into manhood. His English name was Joseph Rael, a true American-Indian shaman from the Pictures Pueblo tribe. He felt that there were few real men left on Mother Earth.

"They are all boys who have yet to become independent from their fathers' fears. Boys are running the world. Boys are causing wars. Boys have taken power while attached to their fathers' fears, their fathers' fathers' fears, and so on. They do not know about sound, light, being and vibration! It is the boys who are destroying this planet!"

One of the most intense times with Beautiful Painted Arrow was releasing all the guilt and shame I had picked up from my father's gruesome experiences in World War II – the torture he saw and participated in with the Japanese and the unspeakable atrocities he experienced in hand-to-hand combat at Okinawa.

The next day with Beautiful Painted Arrow, I was to release all the guilt and shame on my mother's side – she being "illegitimate" by my grandmother being an Indian alcoholic prostitute.

After two weeks of fasting, sweat lodging, being taught and initiated into manhood, I passed my final initiation and learned how to properly dance, sing and most importantly, hear the sacred sounds as a Man. I also received my new name, "RA."

Chapter 20

DEAN RADIN

Professor Dean Radin was one of the few scientists I shared my multidimensional experiences with. I remember being introduced to him by Meegan McFeely, Clarus' PR person in the mid 1990s. He was still at the IONS (Institute of Noetic Sciences) facilities at 101 San Antonio Road in Petaluma. We first met upstairs in his library and spoke of our common missions, then he took me down to his private lab which housed the famous "chamber" (box) he had been using for experiments for several years.

The Chamber is an 8x8x7.5-foot box constructed with various materials to completely block all forms of electromagnetism, including radio, TV and cellular phone signals.

He let me sit inside with the door closed.

Wow! Home. Peace.

> There is a grid comprised of various forms of energy which encompasses the entire earth. It is the aura of the earth.

> Modern scientists often refer to the aura, both human and the earth's, as "The Biofield." In 1993, Professor Beverly Rubik who was on the NIH committee for Alternative and Complementary Medicine research under the Clinton Administration, defined The Biofield as "...a field of energy intimately connected with each organism that holds information central to its higher order of being."

> Each human has its own influence within the Earth's Grid. However, unless an individual human, or group of humans, raise themselves to a higher vibration than the Earth's Grid, all individuals and groups will be primarily influenced by

the Grid.

Throughout history there have been specific places on Earth which have been designed as conjunctive portals for higher dimensional energies sometimes called "Transphase Points." Some of these Earth locations have had structures built on them in the past, like the Great Pyramids and Stonehenge.

Many years ago, the grid portals on the earth changed and the new locations were identified by highly intuitive beings, subtle energy detectors and by other means. The locations are like acupuncture points for the earth. Stimulate any one of these points and all kinds of things connected to that point are influenced.

Over the last one hundred years, and in exponential proportions over the last thirty years, the earth's biofield has been affected in many ways which are not supporting the Highest Potential Blueprint of Earth, and therefore, the Highest Potential Blueprint of Each Human Being. The grid now includes deleterious thought form clusters. As a result, deleterious physical combinations of energy have been able to express on Earth in the forms of pollution of the air, water, plants and food sources, etc. The air, water and food then affects the beings who rely on these energetic clusters for their physical lives.

More important at this time of Earth are the subtle energetic domains which affect our thoughts, emotions, actions and even the degree of accuracy of our five senses.

99.99% of all humans are being significantly influenced by the deleterious thought and energy structures contained in the fourth dimension. However, because of the profound influence now coming from the Divine level, the path toward self-destruction is being altered. Nonetheless, because of the Great Gift of Free Will, human participation is necessary for the Highest Potential of the Awakening.

It is a function of human consciousness. During this time of Earth (the awakening time), raising mass consciousness to its next highest level of potential is necessary. The earth's grid and aura – the earth's biofield – will actually start to change to a more gold color, and thereby each human's aura will also begin to show this. That's why many of the prophecies have called this time, the "Golden Age." It is not a metaphor; it is literal.

When all colors of the Chakras are expressed via their full potential through the Heart center according to the blueprint of this time of Earth, the color will become gold. It is simple frequency physics. By properly combining the seven primary colors of the rainbow – red, orange, yellow, green, blue, indigo and violet – the color gold will appear. Gold is primarily a function of the proper proportions of violet (the seventh Chakra), red (the first Chakra) through green (the fourth, Heart Chakra)...with orange, indigo, yellow and blue as supportive.

"The Golden Age" is a function of the Earth's Grid. The Earth's Grid is constantly being influenced by, 1) The Divine Blueprint: the slowest but most potent wave forms, 2) mass consciousness: the sum total of all individual influences, and 3) individual consciousness.

Wow! Home. Peace. Time seemed to stop while I was in the Chamber at IONS. Dean opened the door and asked how I was doing.

"I'm *not* doing," I said jokingly. "I'm *being!*"

It was not an unfamiliar feeling. It reminded me of the fifth dimension I had often traveled through. You are free and clear, yet you can still sense your boundary, your subtle body and your individuality.

134

"It is in this chamber where we can rule out any invisible electromagnetic wave interference on a person or an experiment. We also can control the temperature, air quality and humidity," Dean informed me.

We spoke for a good length of time about such things as how consciousness can affect matter, and a hotter topic for both of us, how mass consciousness can be raised for the benefit of the earth and every human being. He told me about his "random number generators" and other devices which had been shown to respond to mass consciousness.

After my visions in 2009 I met with Dean and his assistant Leena Michael once again to discuss my theory for raising mass consciousness by somehow reaching 1% of the global population. That was sixty-three million people at the time. We sketched out a project called "Quorum One Percent" or "Q-1%." We would find a way to provide a technology, which had been shown to improve the quality of life for individuals, to sixty-three million people! One of the ideas was a pendant or bracelet that you could pin on your shirt or wear on your wrist with the known field affects. The Q-1% pendants and bracelets would also be made with a short-distance radio signal circuit that would activate a little vibration if another Q-1% device was within 100 feet.

We would start a movement in Consciousness: "The Greatest Experiment in the History of Humanity." If we improve the quality of life for 1% of the human population, would the other 99% be affected? In other words, would the quality of life *everywhere* improve?

We masterminded more. We could set up RNGs (Random Number Generators) in all the major cities, and with constant updates to all Q-1% participants, we could establish a friendly contest: which city can get to 1% the quickest? And, more importantly, what quality-of-life indexes would change and by how much?

Celebrity endorsements would be imperative. We would kick off the campaign after we had at least three major celebrities call a press conference of some kind to announce the experiment. In addition to RNG's, the controls would be established for each major city, such as crime rate, hospital ER admissions, school absenteeism and even local business productivity. Later, I found that statisticians had included in the "Quality of Life Index" such markers as job satisfaction, relationship satisfaction, health, overall well-being and happiness."

Then, an amazing discovery happened which has given us the way to get to even more than 1% – quickly. We had the revelation of how to transmit the Quantum Code Technology to mobile devices, thus enabling us to reach the entire global community. This forms what we call the 1% Challenge, through the One08 Heart+ App.

Chapter 21

MASTERS AMONG US

The first morning Patti and I looked out at Keylakekua Bay, she exclaimed, "They're coming. I feel them!"

"Are you sure?" I asked.

"Absolutely, let's go."

We kayaked out about one half mile and, sure enough, after about fifteen minutes, we spotted them swimming into the bay from the open sea. A chill of energy went up my spine, but I assumed that was because I realized I was actually away from the phones, faxes, emails and sales reports and was in a beautiful place far from home. Or was I?

I had met Patti about 4 years prior to going to Hawaii with her. We instantly recognized each other when we first met but not in one of those clichéd ways. It was deeper, humbling, and profound. She had had her own near death experiences and had seen the same symbols I had in 1979. When I met her in 1991 I needed no further confirmation about the other planes of existence nor of the symbols. Nevertheless, it was as if a long-lost love had been found. We would help each other with our human existence. Our relationship was not romantic or sexual, yet it was an extreme brightness of Light and Love.

We didn't speak much about the symbols or even the higher dimensions. After we compared our notebooks and reveled over the similarities, we closed our eyes and traveled into the other dimensions together. This was the first time in my life I had done anything like this with another human being. We learned to find and meet each other within the fifth dimension. Together we could maintain consciousness and remember more especially in the sixth and higher domains.

Soon after I met her she insisted that we travel to Keylakekua to swim with the wild dolphins. It took over three years, but we were finally on the rocky beach.

Patti shouted, "Let's go in," and as we hurriedly put on our snorkels and fins, the dolphins swam even closer to our boat. Patti jumped in before me, then I did. But after ten seconds I realized water was rapidly filling up my mask and then going up my nose. I snorted and coughed in a very city-boy manner and struggled back to the boat.

The waves were swelling and the wind started blowing. I also kept feeling my wedding ring slipping off my finger; I was afraid to open my hand. As I reached the boat and grabbed the side, Patti saw what was going on and returned to my aid only to find that she hadn't the slightest clue why my mask was leaking.

During this ordeal the dolphins never left. They just kept circling and I got the feeling that they were highly entertained by what they were observing.

Patti had the idea to exchange masks and when that didn't work I decided to get back in the boat to figure out the problem. "You first," I shouted. Patti, of course, hopped up and positioned herself in the boat without a problem, but when I tried to swing my leg over something happened and I flipped the boat completely over spilling the camera, our drinking water, lunches, hats, shoes, paddles, life coats...and she and I into the ocean.

Even though I frantically raced to gather everything up, yelling instructions to Patti, "Hold the stuff, I'll flip the boat," I couldn't help but notice two dolphins side-by-side, swimming very close by. There was no longer a feeling of amusement coming from them, but of concern. I was able to flip the boat back and we got all the stuff and ourselves safely back in.

I said to Patti that because I couldn't find a good place to safely store my ring, I would stay in the boat and she could go in. She smiled and after resting a bit, jumped back in and swam with the dolphins for at least forty-five minutes. But that's her story.

On the way back to our beach house, we saw another lone dolphin surfacing ahead of us. This was odd as dolphins usually stay together in their pod.

This one dolphin was all by himself and after zigzagging in front of us several times, it disappeared. A few minutes later we thought there were more dolphins approaching the boat from a different direction. We both got excited again and Patti put on her flippers to jump in once again. But something didn't feel quite right, so she waited and we just watched the movement in the water for what seemed to be a very long time. "Are these dolphins?"

As soon as I asked the question, Patti screamed, "They're sharks!"

"Are you kidding?" I asked completely confused as I had remembered reading in the tourist journal that sharks were extremely rare in that bay. Rare didn't mean never.

So we raced back to the house with the shark experience just about overshadowing our dolphin encounter. Every local expert on the subject we asked said that it was extremely rare and most didn't believe us. We could tell by the way they said, "Sharks you say, uh-huh. Big ones? Well don't worry now folks, just enjoy yourselves, and aloha!"

That night as I was drifting off to sleep, I relived the feeling the dolphins gave off as I struggled with my snorkel, and also the way those two dolphins looked at me when I was struggling in the water. But especially how the one dolphin seemed to try to communicate to us about the sharks.

It wasn't until a few days later that I had my life-changing experience.

It was an unusually cold morning and Patti had not yet felt their presence. But I was bound and determined since I finally figured out how to snorkel at a place up the coast the day before. There I had the great pleasure of not only seeing beautiful and colorful tropical fish up close, but also a very old sea turtle, who upon noticing me trailing him, gave me the most nonchalant look I've ever received.

After paddling to where they usually come in, I asked Patti if she felt them. "No, not this morning. They don't come in every morning, you know, and I think this is one of them."

I tried something – I closed my eyes and went to that centered Heart space and asked them if they were coming in.

Immediately, I heard, "Yes."

The immediacy and clarity of this message startled me, but I responded while still in the space, "How long?"

"Within twenty minutes," was the reply.

I didn't tell Patti this as we sat there waiting and looking. After about fifteen minutes she said again, "I don't think they're coming. Not this morning." Right when she said that we both heard the familiar spouting sound emitted when they come up for air. We looked to our right and there they were, swimming right by us about forty feet from the kayak.

I quickly put my snorkel on and jumped into the water, swimming their way. Within a few minutes I saw them down below, swimming playfully. This was the same pod we had seen earlier – two babies that loved to jump (a beautiful spinning jump that has given this breed of dolphins their name), and one who loved to flap his or her tail just on the surface of the water.

140

What impressed me more than anything were their voices. The chatter was amazing and very loud. I went to my Heart, letting go of my mind's interpretation; I knew something much more significant. It was as if every dolphin understood every other dolphin in the pod at the same time.

Before too long they quickly swam away; I completely lost any sight of them and the ocean was silent. I kept swimming without really knowing where I was going. For some reason, I didn't want to stop and look above water to get my bearings.

Any ocean swimmer knows that underwater it's very easy to get mixed up about which way is toward the shore, etc.

I could see only dark blue-green.

The day before, I had the delight in swimming with the dolphins and seemingly communicating via a set of sacred symbols that I broadcast out from my Heart Chakra. It had, I thought, immediately attracted two older dolphins (the "elders" as I began to call them) that swam with me a long while. I felt their amused interest but nothing more.

So I tried broadcasting the symbols once again. There is one symbol in particular that had elicited the greatest response the day before, so instead of scanning through more than one symbol, I focused only on this one. At the same time, I began thanking the dolphins for the opportunity to swim in their waters and offered myself to them in an unconditional sense.

I was still swimming blindly, but again for some reason I refused to look up out of the water.

All of a sudden I heard, "Swim more to the right." I couldn't believe it! Were they directing me to them? I followed the instructions and after a while heard, "Now more to the left.

No, too much, more straight forward. Now make a sharp right..."

This kept on for quite a while and then I heard, "Now, keep going straight. You'll see."

Less than a minute later I heard their acoustic sounds and saw at least fifty dolphins swimming easily about thirty feet in front of me and about fifty feet below. I was thrilled and amazed, but then something else happened – more fundamental.

I felt one of the most powerful waves of unconditional Love I have ever felt since visiting the seventh dimension!

As I stopped swimming and just floated, they all began to come to me. I saw the two babies and the elders, and felt some of their different but distinct personalities.

But all of them radiated this extraordinary unconditional Love. It was an unmistakable field. I recognized it immediately.

Just like the glorious beings, The Christ Masters, who I had visited in the higher dimensions in the 1980's, these dolphins were generating the same Field.

So I floated with my snorkel hose just above the water, looking down at them.

I decided to go back to one of my symbols and almost before I broadcast it out, I heard, "Yes, we know all about these symbols. Very good."

The two elder dolphins that had swam with me the day before came by. I was absolutely amazed. I then asked via my mind directly in English, "Can you understand me?"

"Yes."

"But how if I communicate in English?"

"By way of The Universal Translator," they said.

I asked, "Is it along the lines of my experience of 'metaharmonics'?" Again the two elders swam close by.

"Somewhat," they answered.

All of a sudden I realized that I was getting very cold (that bay has various cold and warm areas) and I decided to integrate the whole experience to that point. I finally looked above water to see where Patti was, and saw her about twenty-five feet from me, having followed me in the boat. She had a huge smile on her face. I gave her the okay sign and went face down once again, but I was now shivering with cold.

They were swimming away. I asked permission to follow them. They said, "Yes," and for about five minutes I followed them.

Soon the water became very warm and the dolphins stopped swimming away and started to play again. Could it be they actually picked up on the fact that I was cold? Before I could even consciously ask the question I heard, "The cold makes no difference to us, but it does to you, so we are here."

The elders were still together swimming back and forth from me. I thought to myself, "This is amazing." How blessed I was. This is a golden opportunity for me to learn. So, I asked a few personal questions.

Their response, "Be gentle with yourself; remember you are always in a flow in life...and Play."

As the dolphins continued to swim around me I thought what on Earth am I going to do to play with these magnificent beings? The only thing I could think of was to start singing.

"You are my sunshine...my only sunshine. You make me happy...when skies are gray..."

They were delighted and immediately a couple of large adults approached me, although the young ones seemed to enjoy watching. I noticed one of the adults that came forward had a discolored fluke right at the joint. I thought maybe it was an injury.

He turned to me and I heard "Play."

The discolored fluke turned out to be an ocean leaf. One would "grab" the leaf with his fluke, swim with it for a while then drop it off, and as it began to sink the other would swirl down and catch it and then repeat the game.

I swam for the leaf while still singing. One came up to me before I could get it and circled me. I kept rotating with him keeping eye contact. I'll never forget the feeling of this, the eye contact, his dolphin smile and the amazing clicking and clacking sounds he was making.

He must have spun me around at least a half dozen times before he went for the leaf and dove out of sight, only to return a few seconds later with two leafs, one on each fluke! He approached me again, along with the other dolphin who had started the game.

At this point I noticed two other snorkelers swimming frantically toward us. I had read in the dolphin literature that dolphins don't like snorkelers who swim "at" them, wanting a thrill and needing an experience.

At first I was disappointed that these people entered my special space, which immediately stopped the leaf game. But I could not hold on to a negative thought.

The dolphins changed their "field" to compassion and understanding. They gave the swimmers the same amused look and feeling that they gave me during my first haphazard experience with my snorkel and tipping the boat.

144

I then joined with the Dolphins' Field and felt complete compassion for the frantically swimming folks.

When I went back under the water, the dolphins were retreating and the two snorkelers were racing after them. I floated down a bit and thanked the dolphins for this extraordinary experience and held my hands to my heart.

After a few seconds they were out of my sight, so I started swimming back to the boat – when out of the corner of my eye, I saw the two elders coming back to me. They paused briefly and looked at me.

"We love all life," was what I heard and they then dove deep out of sight.

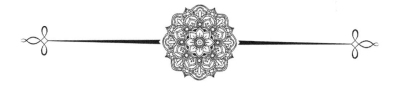

Chapter 22
LOVE

The Ultimate Purpose of Humanity is to Realize Love – without any reason, need, expectation or condition of any kind.

The Ultimate Purpose of Love cannot be attained by effort, intention or achievement.

The Ultimate Purpose of Love is realized suddenly, when all previous thoughts, concepts, emotions and beliefs are repositioned by our Heart's innate intelligence.

Thoughts, emotions and physical realities are always subordinate to The Heart.

There are many factors which affect our lives, such as where our attention is placed from moment to moment, what thoughts we are favoring, who we spend our time with, what we eat, how we treat ourselves and others, and how much pain or bliss we are in. All of these things influence us, but none of these things ever cause us to realize Love.

There is never a local cause for Love. Love is what is prior, beneath and always One with Light, Truth and Real Happiness.

Love defies polarities. Love collapses all paradox. Love is The Heart.

I pondered the concept of love from as far back as I can remember. One of the cool things about my family is that "I love you" was said a lot. Whenever we would go to bed, we all told each other we loved them. Whenever we would finish a phone call we would end with "I love you."

When I was with Jing and the nature spirits, I felt that I was always receiving goodness, compassion, understanding and help in many ways from them, depending upon my circumstances. In their presence I always felt better, physically as well as emotionally. I felt their "lightness." My physical body always seemed to feel better while I was with them. The physical sensations I had with them were often "tingly" and I would get the kind of chills we get when we are inspired or feel something that really makes us happy. Happy feelings – I thought that was Love. The energies in the back yard changed when springtime arrived. Springtime was a time when many of the trees and plants began to flower.

> We can say that the fulfillment of a plant is its blossoming flower which naturally is found following all the previous stages of development – seed, root, sprout, stem and leaf. The time of the flowering can be anticipated, prophesized and even predicted based on the observance of the seasons, the environmental influences and the right amount of sunlight and water. But the actual moment of the blossoming, or even if there is a blossoming at all, is always governed by its own innate Laws. There is no separation between one flower's innate Law and the intelligence of the entire Cosmic Domain.

> When the plant is ready to blossom into a flower, subtle signals are released. The codes of nature for the blossoming itself that had been dormant up to that point suddenly become active. All around the garden, the subtle (faster-than-light) nature spirits, elementals and devas are all alerted.

It was different with my family. I felt a certain association with them at times which included a "safe" zone of comfort and security. I felt loved in those moments, but most often their own fears and judgments about themselves and others were too much for any of us to even attempt finding the "safe zone." I've no doubt that we loved each other as much as we were able, but springtime didn't change the quality of love. Perhaps humans respond to a different type of season?

Instead of the "lightness of being" I felt with Jing and the others, I began to define love in terms of emotions and strong sensual feelings once I reached puberty. My love for others became based on my physical, emotional and mental propensities. If I felt good, then I could love freely. If I was in pain, my love for others was motivated by my search for some good feeling, some release or relief of pain.

"He/She loves me" was associated with the emotions of elation and personal happiness. "He/She doesn't love me" became the emotions of sadness and personal despair. I quickly noticed how short-lived these emotions were. Anger would quickly turn to sadness, sadness to despair, despair to inspiration, inspiration to renewed hope...and on and on.

Somewhere in my teens I heard of the concept of unconditional love. I pondered this concept in all aspects of my waking state of consciousness. What was the conditional expectation of me saying "I love you" to my mother? The condition was that I wanted to be loved by her, to be safe in her presence. What was the conditional expectation of saying "I love you" to my girlfriend? I wanted to be able to hold her, to be held by her, to enjoy life with her and to be sexual in one form or another. And so it went that whenever I thought I was loving, I would later reflect and identify conditions for that so-called love.

In high school one of our required reading books was *The Lord of the Flies* by William Golding. Reading that book confirmed my pessimistic viewpoint of humanity. For those of you who don't know the plot, it's basically about a group of boys who survive a nuclear war and wind up on an island by themselves. Despite the education they had received before the disaster, their attempts at self-governance fail miserably and the book ends with the boys devolving to a state of savagery.

I asked the teacher, Mrs. Lokes, why such a book was required reading. She became very emotional, and answered something like, "Because we should all be aware of what lurks underneath so-called civilized life." While she was talking to me I couldn't help but notice a sour red auric color coming from her throat chakra. The statement, whether it was true or not, was her need and her agenda. It was her need to convince me, the class and anyone who would bring the subject up – that evil was fundamentally a part of us all. This was her agenda. Although she loved her students, her personal unresolved pain from whatever happened in her childhood had evolved into strong beliefs, and may have even motivated her to become a teacher – to *teach* us all about that evil.

I remember all the students' mood after finishing Golding's book. We were depressed! And we felt afraid for our future. What would happen if we were the ones that someday would wind up as the only humans left stranded on some island? I guess we assumed that because this book was such a big deal in school, it was some kind of warning about our true nature.

The same color I saw in Mrs. Lokes' throat when she became emotional, not only about *The Lord of the Flies*, but about most anything...I also saw in the throats of the evangelical minsters during my stint as a born-again Christian. Such fury of emotion coming from the minister quickly stimulated the same fury of emotion in the congregation and soon everyone was shouting "Jesus!" or "Praise God!" or "Amen!" Emotions stirred up in groups become much more powerful and effective in influencing others – with their agendas.

Sometimes the emotional movements were very positive – like what Martin Luther King did toward civil rights. It all depends upon where people are at in their consciousness. If emotions were what all people thought they were, the emotions were used to change them – for good things as well as destructive things.

I was also fascinated with Hitler who persuaded the German and other European countries to dismiss their basic sense of loving others, and switch to killing them instead. His speeches and writings were very emotional. He also convinced the minds of people that there were two kinds of people on the earth – superior ones and inferior ones. My father had fought and killed because of this.

I soon concluded that unconditional love did not exist in everyday life and had not existed for a long time. I looked for it everywhere but always saw blatant personal agendas. I also saw sour red colors in people's auras when they spoke of love. I figured the true meaning of *Love* had been lost by humanity and overshadowed with agendas of the personality. It was replaced with some kind of sought-after need to fulfill "our kind" and at worst, by greed – even within our own mindsets of "our kind" of people.

Nevertheless, I also continued to believe that true Love was a field of energy that permeated within and from Nature itself in spite of our personal agendas. By the time I started college I had read and studied spiritual literature including scriptures from Eastern, Western and American Indian cultures. They all spoke of Love, but it wasn't the love that I saw around me in daily life.

I concluded that there needed to be a revival, like when Jesus came, or Buddha or even lesser known religious figures incarnated on planet Earth. I wondered if a Jesus or Buddha would incarnate or reincarnate in my lifetime.

In the fall of 1973 something altered my pessimistic view of the human race.

Hot Ice, my rock band, had a recurring gig at the San Francisco Presidio Officer's Club every Friday and Saturday night. Harold, Danny, Steve and I would arrive promptly on Friday night at 8:00PM to set up for our first set beginning at 9:00PM. We played four sets ending at 1:00AM – unless there was a demand from the crowd to continue, in which case the bartender would give us a signal that we would get paid more. The bar had to be closed by 2:00AM according to California law. If we had been given the signal, the bartender would hysterically give us another signal at 1:45AM to stop all the music and then he'd scream out on our PA system, "LAST CALL" in a very militaristic tone. This would then be followed by a rush to the bar and the three waitresses scrambling to get the drinks distributed before 2:00AM. As long as you had your drink in a glass before 2:00AM, you could take as long as you wanted to drink it. Sometimes *Hot Ice* was there well past 3:00AM.

At least one of the waitresses had to stay until the very end. Of the three, Nancy was the shyest. She didn't wear her skirts so high, nor did she wear as much make-up as the other two. She was the one I was attracted to most.

It must have been past 3:00AM and it was only Nancy, the bartender and *Hot Ice* left at the Presidio Officer's Club. My ears were ringing from our five sets, each set louder than the last. I remember those days well, and I can say that there's nothing like the feeling of being in a club where over a hundred people had stomped out whatever inhibitions they once had prior to the alcohol, rock, flirting and screaming at the top of their lungs, "More, more, more!" The music, alcohol and sexual atmosphere provided the permission they needed for their temporary happiness and exhilaration. Their pain had been temporarily overridden; the frenzy of their dance had superimposed itself over their day-to-day problems and their lives' confusions.

Then, after the final announcement was made, there was no more music, no more people, no flirting and no stomping.

All except for *Hot Ice*, the bartender and Nancy on that night. There was a special bonding of the six of us after so many hours of intensity. As far as there being one girl left in the room, it was the perfect romantic set-up for any of us. Any one of us could have gone home with Nancy, but as fate would have it, it was me.

She and I literally ran into each other after coming out of the restrooms. Even the signs on the restroom doors that night seem to invite sexual encounters – MEN on the right, WOMEN on the left – in large letters.

We stopped in the hallway positioned under our appropriate signs, squinting at each other, our eyes still adjusting to the bright lights outside of the club.

"Hi, Nancy," I said with as much of a manly voice as I could muster.

"Hi, Bob," she said. Although she quickly looked down, she didn't move. It was a signal, I thought!

"Quite a night, eh?

"Yea, so many people," she chimed.

She had an accent that I couldn't quite make out. In the light I could see her dark brown eyes. I had no choice but to ask, "Would you like me to take you home?"

To my surprise she said, "Yes." I later learned she didn't even own a car, and would normally walk home or get a ride home from one of the other waitresses.

It was 3:30AM now. I bid farewell to my bandmates who all gave me that look guys give each other when a "pick-up" had occurred. "You scored!" "Lucky!" "Right-on dude!" etc. Their

152

looks angered me. They had no clue what was really going on. I was searching for *love*, you jerks!

She lived in one of those distinct San Francisco Victorian row houses – top level. I followed her up the three flights of stairs and followed her into her home. The house smelled wonderful from the incense she burned, and every bit of her belongings and furniture felt amazing to me – so unlike the furniture I grew up with in San Lorenzo. This place felt so right and comfortable.

Nancy politely thanked me for the ride, walked me to the door and said good-bye.

What?!

I then said one of the bravest things I've ever said, "Nancy, do you mind if I spend the night with you?"

"Bob, I'm not one of those girls you musicians screw whenever you want. I thought you would be different."

"I am different, Nancy! No sex, I promise!"

"You will not be able to do that. I know men! I only have one bed, no couch."

"I am capable. Please, let's just go to bed," I suggested genuinely.

Perhaps because she was so tired, she allowed me to stay. And then, what I had been searching for happened in a way I had never anticipated or expected. We both took showers, separately. I came out with my same clothes on and she wearing a thick robe. She looked beat and so sad. She then went to her turntable and put on a record. I was transfixed at what I heard. This wasn't rock, these were songs sung in a different language that seemed to beg for what once used to be.

"What is this?"

She told me it was music from her homeland, and that she was born and raised in Israel. When the wars broke out, she had scraped up just enough money to get on a cargo boat from Gaza to San Francisco. She slept at *Golden Gate Park* for weeks while she went from bar to bar, and club to club looking for work. She was only sixteen years old when all this happened. The manager of the Presidio Officer's Club was also from Israel and gave her the waitressing job from 8:00PM to 2:00AM, plus she worked the restaurant downstairs from 9:00AM to 5:00PM. This was her sixth year in the US without a valid visa or driver's license. She just worked and sent most of her money back home. She was now just twenty-two years old.

It was at this part in her story that she started to weep. The weeping turned into deep and heart-wrenching crying. I held her. I had no desire at that point but to sooth her grief. She tried to say something but couldn't get it out. I held her more and said, "What is it?"

"I'm a bad, bad person."

"No you're not! You're working two jobs and sending money back to your family! How can you be bad?"

"I left my son," she confessed.

"What? You have a son?" The idea of having a child at a young age was surprising to most in my generation. I quickly did the math; her son couldn't be more than seven years old.

"Yes, I am bad. I left him in Israel to be raised by my parents. He was too young to bring to America with me. His father, my husband, was killed in the war."

I picked her up and gently got her to bed and got in with her, with our clothes still on. The folk music was still playing in

154

the background.

She was crying less now, and after a few minutes stopped completely. We lay there listening to the songs of her Israeli home – she longing for her son and family – I longing for love.

Suddenly a ray of sunlight hit my eyes.

"Look!" I said as we both saw the most beautiful sunrise happening outside her bedroom window. We both sat up and looked out without saying a word for several minutes.

"I love him – I love my son so much." Now she was speaking softly, accepting.

Soon we were both completely lost as the sun continued to rise, casting the most amazing red, orange and blue colors through her window. The sun didn't care about us and our longings, I realized. It was simply following its own natural rhythm.

The impression of that moment has stayed with me ever since. For those few moments together, we realized we were more than our emotions, more than our needs, our thoughts and our desires.

I turned from the sunrise and looked at her and for the first time in my life saw the brilliant color and radiance of unconditional Love. It was the purest most beautiful golden celestial light I had ever seen. It was a brightness from *her Heart Chakra*. I could almost see her son receiving this Love, wherever he was in Israel.

We drifted off to sleep as the sun rose and the music played.

Just a few hours later, she kissed me and I woke up. I turned and saw her dressed in her waitress outfit at once reminding me that she had to wait tables at 9:00AM.

"I'll drive you!"

"No," she said firmly. "I want to walk."

Before I could protest, she was down the stairs. I looked out her window and saw her rushing toward the Presidio.

"I'll see you tonight!" I yelled. She turned and waved with a smile.

That night at the gig was surreal for me singing *Maybe I'm Amazed* by Paul McCartney while my eyes searched for Nancy.

> *Maybe I'm amazed at the way you pulled me out of time,*
>
> *And hung me on a line.*
>
> *Maybe I'm a man and maybe I'm a lonely man*
>
> *Who's in the middle of something,*
>
> *That he doesn't really understand.*

When Nancy came close to the dance floor I looked for the golden light in her heart I had seen that morning in such glory. All I saw was the overshadowing color of grief, even when she smiled and winked at me.

We tried doing the "boyfriend-girlfriend" thing for a few months afterwards, but we could never recapture the golden moment. She didn't see The Light but she felt that special sunrise moment as I had. She strongly agreed with me it was real love she had been feeling for her son. I didn't doubt her, but I knew something else was at play – some cosmic orchestration.

I tried everything I could think of to activate her golden light – flowers, poems and conversations of her son and life back in Israel. We would set the alarm to wake up just before sunrise, and position ourselves exactly as we were before on the bed, looking out. We saw some beautiful sunrises and would gasp, but no matter how we tried, the golden light never showed up with Nancy again. We would sometimes just fake it for each other, "Yes, this is it again!" But we knew the truth. Our kisses and love-making were bittersweet. She often would cry afterwards, and after a few nights with her, I would too.

Emotions have a way of taking over our lives most of the time, but for all of us, there *are* special moments that occur when we least expect it. Every once in a while human Hearts glow unhindered and Love is found cradling everything.

> *Everything is ultimately Love – both in activity and in silence. There is great power in this understanding and realization.*
>
> *Our state of awareness and our level of consciousness determines how much of Love can be lived, both in silence and in activity.*
>
> *Since Love is the basis and essence of everything, many aspects of our life can be a doorway into each of our own Power of Love.*
>
> *Emotions become doorways to Love.*
>
> *Thoughts become doorways to Love.*
>
> *Spiritual concepts become doorways to Love.*
>
> *What then is the path to Love?*
>
> *Life.*
>
> *How can we realize greater degrees of Love?*
>
> *By living.*
>
> *What do we do with our thoughts, emotions and beliefs?*
>
> *Love them.*
>
> *How do we Love them?*

Unconditionally.

We love them with no expectations for them to change. We breathe into them without agendas; we love them with all our Hearts.

We then, individually and collectively, become doorways for the mighty Laws of Nature beckoning us towards our next highest level of life.

When we live all emotions, thoughts and body feelings AS Love as opposed to searching for love, then we are free to give to others without need or fear. The codes are now active, the signals have been released – the blossoming of humanity's Hearts and life with all our differences woven within the common thread of all our hearts has begun.

If you have read this, you have joined us in the becoming. Your consciousness has resonated with both the hope and reality of the higher Power of Love. Now is the Time.

Thank you.

I was twenty-one years old when one Friday night at the Presidio, Nancy had been replaced by another bar girl. "Where is Nancy?" I asked. The bartender said she just stopped showing up for work that week and he couldn't get ahold of her. "I think she caught a boat back to Israel. She was always talking about it."

I never saw her again, but the golden light would come again many times, until even the shimmering gold color would dissolve into pure undifferentiated Light when my breath stopped during those thirty minutes in March of 1979 - about six years later.

And then from a powerful source completely mysterious to my mind, the breath of my body started again.

Just like you reading these words, and me writing, and all human beings living right now, no matter what our beliefs, our political views, our differences, our breath goes out, and then from that same purposeful and all loving power which has been with us since each of our first breaths, it starts again. Notice it now.

We are One with this Love.

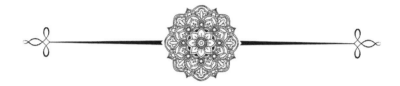

Chapter 23

FEAR TO LOVE –
HEALING THE HEART OF HUMANITY

Our current times are full of immense suffering and cruelty *simultaneous* with the real awakening of millions of human Hearts. More people are understanding and then living a higher love, a more complete compassion, and a greater understanding of the tragedies that have befallen humanity.

Our collective Hearts are connecting more clearly to our collective souls' next highest level of evolution – our next highest level of potential. We are connecting to the blueprint for the awakening of humanity.

There is a raising of consciousness influenced by natural forces many times more powerful than humanity's darkness. These forces shape the next step in human evolution, just like anything that is evolving; the stem to the flower, the caterpillar to the butterfly; the acorn to the oak and many other examples we've all heard of.

For me it was the reality of pure Light in 1979. In the prologue of this book I wrote that the Light dims whenever I speak or write about it. The Light's dimness will only now reach its full brightness when *your* pure light, *your* truth, resonates with mine and just a small percentage of the rest of the human race.

Our minds will always find reasons why this cannot happen or why it is impossible. All that is needed is a few more of our hearts to stir in addition to any thought or feeling we may be having in this moment. One by one, little by little, and then, as per the same laws which have been governing this entire Universe since the beginning of time, there will be a rapid and sudden shift.

A "quantum jump" physicists call it. For most of us it will be a collective "ah-ha!" This "ah-ha" will confirm all the "ah-ha's" we've had in our pasts. But more profoundly, it will ground the collective "ah-ha" in a new reality. This is simply the law.

There is current evidence that there are enough people ready to make a difference. There is strong evidence that all we need is 1% of the total population to shift things to what Prof William Tiller calls "the SU{2} – Gauge Symmetry" state of life, or what we are calling, a society based in Love not fear – also described as The Maharishi Effect. In the 1960s, Maharishi Mahesh Yogi claimed that just 1% of people practicing Transcendental Meditation in a given area could have a profound impact on their environment. The twelve scientific studies done by MIU also support the fact that only 1% is needed to create the shift in global consciousness. The results show that the "Quality of Life Index" was significantly improved across several cities worldwide. Quantum Code Technology (QCT™) is what we call the technology that amplifies the array of information packets designed within the blueprint of evolution that we will activate using the Heart+ App and the 1% Challenge.

There are certain information packets that are active for humanity. The only difference between the comparison to caterpillars and flowers is that the activation of the human heart has never been completed – at least since the beginning of our known history. It is now more than ever, ready for completion.

QCT removes the interferences effecting both our physical hearts and our spiritual hearts. QCT reveals what is already there – a stronger physical heart, and a clearer spiritual Heart with greater access to Love, Compassion and Understanding.

The Heart's ability to Love will not be an irresponsible allowance of terror or violence, because when 1% of the population is given the chance to live an awakened life – with their Heart Chakras in field resonance with millions of others, positive change in global attitudes and solutions are inevitable.

QCT empowers holistic decision-making. The evolved Heart's vibration is always holistic, always attuned to both "them" and "us." Although QCT reveals and allows the already present love, appreciation, and compassion we all have, it also empowers the Collective Heart for massive coherence and global problem solving. The awakening Heart is not passive, but contains a tremendous energy and power to transform one state of existence to another.

Just like the garden plant's innate power to forge the changes required to go from a seed to a sprout, a sprout to a stem, to a bud, and then to a fully blossomed flower...the human Heart has already been created with the built-in Power of Love for the transformation we've all been hoping and praying for. From a basis of fear and separatism to a basis of Love and a co-creative life together.

The Power of Love is real, and with enough alignment of sympathetic hearts from real people, mass transformation must occur. This Love is the same Love a mother and father tap into when their child is in trouble. It is automatic and massively powerful.

I believe that only Seventy-Five million people; literally 1% of the global population is enough. Seventy-five million will effect the 7.5 billion beings on our planet because there are laws of physics behind this.

QCT has found a way to transmit the 108 sacred natural energies via the Heart+ App on all smartphones. The 108 life supporting field codes are the fundamental "bedrock" of the human biofield. QCT is the result of novel processes, which identify, convert and harness these life supporting codes. In the case of QCT interacting with human biofields, the Heart+

App is generating the 108 ideal life supporting codes to improve the quality of life on all levels. The codes are already part of the foundation of the biofield, and therefore, the Heart+ App simply enhances and supports the innate intelligence for maximum life potential. All you have to do is download the Heart+ App and you will be helping yourself and all of humanity move from fear to Love.

QCT empowers the Heart's own vibration as a function of our birthright. The Heart has always known the answers; it's been trying to speak to us for a long time. But when noise rose to a certain point, the Heart Song was drowned out – overridden. We immediately felt fear because of this. We began to fear everything, even our understanding of Love.

In 2017 a groundbreaking scientific study was published in *The Journal of Alternative and Complementary Medicine* on Quantum Code Technology. If we reconnect our Hearts with the vibrations of Nature itself (the One08 Quantum Codes), we can heal. More profoundly, we can realize that the Heart's Love is still there, previously latent, but ready to heal ourselves, our families, our communities – and our world. We are not healing mass diseases or physical sickness, although that may happen, we are healing our troubled souls and sending strong signals of Love, Compassion and intelligent decision-making to the other 99% of the world. WE are the 1%. WE are the minority with the greatest amount of power for the Good.

What's even more exciting is that our Hearts are wanting to find each other, not only to recognize the look in each other's eyes, and to feel each other's community, but to utilize the power of our collective Hearts together for true global change.

This is our golden opportunity. Together we are finding our true home; not up or away from earth, not discarding our individual bodies or personalities, but because of our unique individualities, right here, right now, incarnated physically together. And when 1% of us "get it" the 99%

will automatically have an easier time for their own next highest level of good.

This is our responsibility and a gift - ALL our hearts together, united with each heart individually.

Join us at www.healtheworldproject.com to be a part of the 1% and celebrate the awakening of global mass consciousness with infinite possibilities for each of us and our entire human-ity. Let's make this world a better place for us and our children with unconditional love for all life to flourish on Planet Earth.

With Unconditional Love,

Robert Odus Williams

One08 Inc is a mobile app company that transmits the Quantum Code Technology™ (QCT) through the Heart+ App via the Apple and Android App stores. QCT has been scientifically shown through double blind gold standard scientific studies to lower your stress by 30.2% and improve your heart health. Just by doing so you will also be a part of our global 1% Challenge.

Our mission is to have more than 1% of the global population using Quantum Code Technology™ as we believe the result will be a positive advance for the mass consciousness of humanity. Ultimately we believe this can create a fundamental healing for our planet and make this world a better place for us and our children.

Please download and use the Heart+ App.

Just leave it on all the time, as it doesn't waste your battery life or use any data while it broadcasts the QCT. Tell your family and friends to download the app and to be a part of the 1% Challenge too. Together as ONE we can make real global change happen.

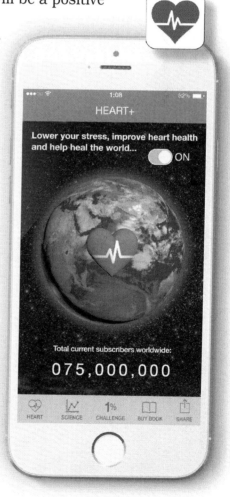

NOTES

NOTES

NOTES

45690446R00104

Made in the USA
San Bernardino, CA
14 February 2017